Endorsements

Leah Adams writes to glorify God and bring the Scriptures to life. She does exactly that in *James: Recipe for a Living Faith*. Leah's authentic writing is always truth-telling, making the gospel even more beautiful. The recipe found in this Bible study is one we all need and can use for living a life filled with a living faith. Thank you, Leah, for allowing God to use your voice to guide us on this journey of faith.

Karen Barrows
Compassion International, Speaker Relations Director

Through her writing, Leah is available and transparent to open up her treasure chest called life. It's full of wisdom, life experiences, and revelation that have challenged and encouraged lives all over the world. Lean in, take notes, and apply the wisdom revealed in the Book of James. It's like a cool drink of water in the desert, continually refreshing those who will engage with it.

Mike Medori
Pastor, Vertical Church of the Mountains, Blairsville, Georgia

We also recommend Leah's other Bible study,

***Hebrews: A Better Blend*, by Warner Press:**

This (*HeBrews: A Better Blend*) has been a great study! One of the best I've ever done or led.

Lisa Pickens
Bible Study Leader

As a wonderful, creative writer, Leah Adams managed to magically place herself in the midst of our women's Bible study group each week as we studied *HeBrews: A Better Blend*. We could almost imagine her sitting among us explaining and interpreting the characters, history, and fascinating details of a book that might have easily been daunting. Leah became a teacher and a friend to us. She was honest, genuine, and we trusted her. Open your front door and invite her in—you will learn, laugh, and long remember the lessons God has inspired her to teach you.

Debbi Brightbill
Bible Study Leader

Leah C. Adams

JAMES

Recipe for a Living Faith

A Six-week Bible Study

Warner Press, Inc.
Warner Press and Warner Press logo are trademarks of Warner Press, Inc.
James: Recipe for a Living Faith
Written by Leah Adams

Requests for information should be sent to:
Warner Press, Inc.
2902 Enterprise Drive
Anderson, IN 46013
www.warnerpress.org

Editors: Karen Rhodes, Robin Fogle
Cover by Curtis Corzine
Design and layout by Katie Miller
ISBN: 9781684341757
Printed in USA

warner press®

MADE IN THE USA

CONTENTS

FOREWORD

We live in an age of epic distractions. While knowledge may be power, the Information Age created a new complication for us—information overload. Most of us face this problem daily via cool-looking screens we carry in our pockets. Yet long before smart phones and the digital lifestyle appeared on the horizon, James spoke wisdom to anyone who would listen: Be doers of the word, and not hearers only (James 1:22). *Information is great, but even the best information, the Word of God, is incomplete without action. Action is the real currency of the twenty-first century. Sorry, Bitcoin.*

I know Leah Adams to be a doer of the Word. My family and I worked for many years as missionaries in a difficult, restricted nation. Leah frequently reached out to us with prayer and emotional support. Although I know she would prefer I not share this particular tidbit of information, I think it's important for you to know she also funded local ministry projects for our underground seminary students. She lives the Christian life from a position of action, not simply knowledge.

When Leah asked me to write the foreword for her new study on James, I of course felt honored, but I was mostly excited at the chance to see her manuscript in advance. She is a gifted teacher who brings her Southern charm to the pages of this study. Leah skillfully invites us to engage with the Book of James through stories, examples, and background information, all while teaching personal Bible study skills. You might just become a better cook too, because she shares some of her favorite recipes throughout the study. All these inviting components offer a great excuse to kick the guys out for a ladies' Bible study night, if you ask me.

But let's face it: James has some hard things to say. He's not exactly touchy-feely. Leah matches James step-for-step and isn't afraid to tackle these difficult issues, which is one of the reasons I find her study so refreshing. She addresses sin for what it is, and her topical approach takes some of the hard truths in James and provides a broader biblical context to them. The end result is a rich, gospel-centered approach for living out God's commands in our daily lives.

History has yet to say whether our generation of women will be one that gathered around screens and at conferences to consume information about the Word of God...or a generation of women who took massive action on the Word that was implanted. My prayer for you, as you turn the pages of this study, is that you will allow the Word to transform you from the inside out. Let it move you to action and affect the way you speak to your children, the way you care for the stranger, the way you get honest before God about your sin. The twenty-first century needs a generation of women who take action. Let's be those women.

Arabah Joy
Author, Blogger, and Online Mentor at arabahjoy.com

PREFACE

A Word from Leah…

There I sat, minding my own business.

I had no writing project ongoing, nor was I writing with any regularity on my blog. My writing mojo had seemed to depart, and I was unsure if it would ever return. And I was not unhappy about it.

Then, in mid-November 2018, an email popped into my inbox. The email was from my sweet editor at Warner Press, Karen Rhodes, whom I had not heard from for a long time. The subject line read, "Hey, woman, how are you?" Yay, a let's catch-up email from Karen.

I opened the email, and in the very first paragraph, she dropped a nuclear bomb on me.

"I'm writing to ask if you would consider writing another Bible study for us."

Say what??? I reread the sentence. Yep, that's what it said. She also told me that my previous Bible study, HeBrews: A Better Blend was still selling well, and they wanted another "Leah" study. You could have knocked me over with a feather. Write another Bible study? Hmmmm…

I asked her if I could pray about it for a few days and get back with her. She agreed, and so I did. After several days the Lord told me to say "yes" to writing a Bible study on the Book of James. What you hold in your hands is that "yes."

I have prayed like a crazy woman over this Bible study. Please understand, I always pray as I write, but this time I had no words to put on paper. If this Bible study were going to be written, the responsibility for it would be on God's Holy Spirit. He called me to it, and He MUST equip me with words. He was, and is, and always will be faithful, praise His holy name!

So many people deserve a shout out for supporting and encouraging me as I write. One group of people rises to the top, however.

Karen Rhodes and the team at Warner Press: Thank you for entrusting this book to me. You do your jobs with distinction, professionalism, and vision. It is my privilege to, once again, partner with you on a book. I pray this study encourages many to live life with renewed determination to look more like Jesus to those who circle around their lives.

And to Jesus: You are the reason I have words to tap out on a keyboard. You are the reason I live and move and breathe. You are my very best Friend, and I will go to my grave praising You for Your willingness to be my substitute on the cross. When God sees me, He sees me through Your blood. I am chosen, redeemed, forgiven, adopted…a precious daughter of the King. There are no words to express the gratefulness and adoration I feel for You.

Leah

INTRODUCTION

"How do I know if God is speaking to me?"

This is such a common question among Christ-followers, and I'm pretty sure it is not a question exclusive to twenty-first century Christians. After Jesus died on the cross, rose on the third day, and left earth for heaven, those who follow Christ live by faith, and listen for the still, small voice of the Holy Spirit for guidance.

You might ask, "In what ways does God speak to us?"

There are several. God speaks to us as we are praying to Him, through other people, books, music, nature, but His voice is most apparent in Scripture. Scripture is God's heart for His people poured out in ink.

Another common question among Christians is, "How do I live like Jesus?"

The entire canon of Scripture has a redemptive red thread woven throughout. From Genesis to Revelation, we find the most excellent love story ever told, the story of how God made possible a restored relationship with humans by sending Jesus to pay the debt for our sin. A debt we would never be able to pay.

There is wisdom for life in each book of the Bible, but none, other than Proverbs, even comes close to James in wisdom and encouragement for our daily walk with Jesus. My prayer is that through this Bible study, you will hear God's voice offering instruction for living a life that reflects Jesus.

The fact that you have chosen this Bible study tells me that you, dear friend, want your journey on this groaning earth to shout *Christ in [me], the hope of glory* (Colossians 1:27). You have come to the right place. James will be our mentor throughout this study. He will encourage us at times while trampling our toes at other times. The Book of James is practical, engaging, and short enough to read in one sitting. It is full of commands and wisdom born of life experience. James held nothing back in his letter because he knew the only way to live is the Jesus way.

After six weeks of sitting at the feet of James, we will come to the end of the study, having read the entire book, but we will not go through it chronologically. The Lord has suggested a topical study of James rather than a chapter-by-chapter, verse-by-verse study. As we dive in, I think you will see why.

What you hold is a six-week Bible study that can be done individually or as a group. (Group studies are wonderful, so find a few friends and dive in together!) Contained within each week of the study are five days of at-home study. Notice I did not use the dreaded H word—homework. Each day of study will require 20–30 minutes of your time. Also included in each week of the study is a memory or meditation verse or verses from James, one from each chapter in the book. I am committing to memorizing all of these, and I hope you will join me. You will find them within each week of the study and also on a page at the back of the book, designed to allow you to cut them out and carry them with you. Something new for me in this study is that I have included topics for further study in some of the days of at-home work. The "For Further Study" section is for those who can't get enough and want to go deeper. You are free to do it or not, and there is no condemnation for choosing not to do it.

God's Word is living and active and has the power to change your life. Engage with it, and I promise you will find yourself walking closer to Jesus and looking more like Him. Pinky promise!

I am eager to take this journey with you and will be praying for you. Grab your Bible, a pen, and a heart set on pursuing Christlike living. I will meet you in our first week of study.

WEEK ONE

James: His Life and Legacy

Mentor.

From loads of personal experience as both a mentor and a mentee over the past ten years, I have learned that a mentor is an older or older-in-the-faith person who comes alongside a younger or younger-in-the-faith person and offers encouragement, instruction, correction, and accountability for a specific task, or for life in general.

It is my privilege to mentor women in life and the kitchen. Often I bring women and girls into my kitchen and teach them how to make homemade dishes that will bless their families' tummies. I give them instruction on how to make the recipe and encouragement to go home and try making it themselves. Sometimes a woman will call or text me to find out why a dish she made did not turn out Pinterest worthy. That gives me a teaching moment to correct anything that went awry. No small number of husbands have thanked me for helping their wife cook some tasty dishes.

As you and I walk through our days, our lives should be patterned after the life that Jesus lived while He was on earth. Nowhere do we need a mentor more than in our calling to live like Jesus. God knew that and sovereignly placed the Book of James in Holy Writ. This week we will spend time getting to know our mentor, James, and understand a bit about why he felt compelled to write the book that bears his name.

For this first week's memory verse, you will think I have lost my mind, and that is possible. However, I believe by the time you turn the page on the final day of Week 1 homework, you will completely agree with me that James 1:1 is a perfect memory verse for this week. Write every word of the verse in the space below.

James 1:1

Recipe

I always tell those who pull up to my table that they are our guest the first time they eat with us; after that, they are family. So, the first recipe I would serve to you and James is one that is a favorite with my family and most of the people who have tucked their knees beneath my table.

A dear friend gave me the recipe for Creamy Chicken Enchiladas years ago. I have no idea where it originated, but it is a gem. Creamy Chicken Enchiladas are rich, creamy, comfort food if ever comfort food existed. They are easy to make and can be assembled very quickly. That makes them a total win for weeknight dinners, especially if you use a precooked rotisserie chicken, which I am convinced is a gift from the hand of God.

RECIPE — Creamy Chicken Enchiladas

- 1 tablespoon (or more) **butter**
- 1 medium **onion**, chopped
- 1 4.5 oz. can chopped **green chilies**, drained
- 1 8 oz. package **cream cheese**, softened and cut into large chunks
- 3½ cups chopped, cooked **chicken breast**
- 8 medium sized **flour tortillas**
- 8–10 oz. **Monterey Jack cheese**, shredded (can use Pepper Jack if you like some zing)
- 2 cups **whipping cream**

Preheat oven to 350°F.

Melt butter in a large skillet over medium heat. Add onions and sauté 5 minutes or until onions become translucent. Add green chilies and sauté for 1 minute. Add in cream cheese and chicken, stirring constantly until cream cheese melts.

Spoon 2–3 tablespoons of chicken mixture down center of each flour tortilla. Roll the individual tortillas around the chicken mixture and place in a lightly greased 9 x 13 baking dish, seam side down.

Sprinkle tortillas with Monterey Jack cheese, then drizzle with whipping cream. Cover with foil and bake for 45 minutes.

Ready to begin our journey through James? Let's go!

DAY 1

How do you feel about meeting new people?

Are you excited and eager to learn more about them, or does the thought of meeting someone new cause you anxiety? Do you ask yourself questions such as: *Will they like me? What if I say something stupid? Do we have anything in common or will there be long stretches of uncomfortable silence?*

Allow me to put your mind at ease as we meet James in the pages of Scripture. He will like you, and the two of you will have a lot in common. James will encourage you to keep on keeping on in your walk with Jesus. He will also step on your toes occasionally but in a loving sort of way.

Before we invite James over for a cup of coffee, let's start with a 50,000-foot view of the Book of James.

Who wrote the Book of James?

You might be thinking, "Well, duh, Leah. Everyone knows it was James, the brother of Jesus."

Hold your horses a minute! Other "Jameses" have been tossed around over the centuries as the writer of the Book of James, so let's take a few minutes to consider those.

The name James was used abundantly in the early first century and was a form of the Old Testament name Jacob. Several possible authors of the book have floated to the top over the years simply because they were named James. Only two have been given much credence at all, and only one is widely accepted.

1. James, the brother of John; the sons of Zebedee—one of the three intimate friends of Christ
2. James, the son of Alphaeus—another of the disciples with little known about him
3. James, the father of Judas, the disciple—not Judas Iscariot
4. James, the Less (In *Clarke's Commentary* you will find this James also referred to as James, the son of Alphaeus, #2 above)
5. James, the brother of Jesus

While some commentators ascribe the authorship of this book to James, the son of Zebedee, the majority agree that James, the brother of Jesus, is the author. Many things make this choice of authors sensible, so we will lean into that choice.

FOR FURTHER STUDY

Explore a few commentaries on your own about the issue of the identity of the author of James, as well as the dating of the book.

When was the Book of James written?

As with the issue of author identity, divergent opinions exist regarding the dating of the Book of James. If you ascribe to the idea that James, the brother of Jesus, wrote the epistle, then you will understand that it had to be written before A.D. 62 when James was martyred, according to the historian, Josephus. Some believe it was written near the end of James' life, while others think the book was written between A.D. 45 and A.D. 50.

With all of that as background, I want us to spend the remainder of our time today learning about the man, James. We will accomplish this through a character study. Each of the scriptures below reference James, the Lord's brother, in some way. Look up each reference and note the context in which James is mentioned, either directly or inferred.

Matthew 13:54–58

John 7:1–5

Acts 1:12–14 (Careful! There is more than one reference to men named "James" mentioned here.)

Acts 15:13–22

Acts 21:17–18

Galatians 1:18–19

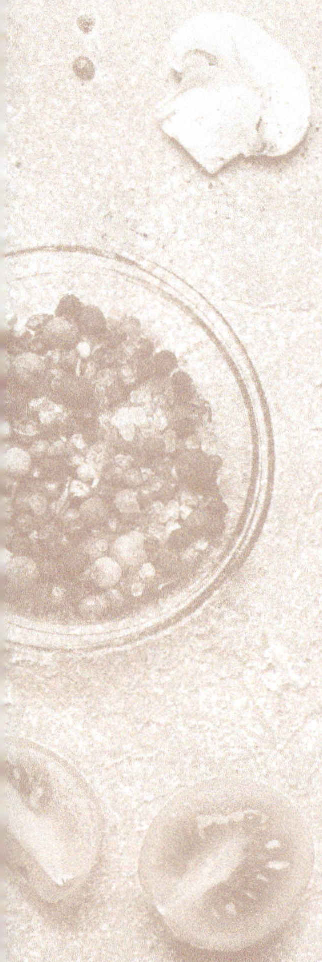

Now that you have put together facts about James, in the space below, write an introduction for James as if you were introducing him to an audience. (There is no right answer for this. It merely helps you put together a character profile of the man.)

Great work today! Every moment you spend in Scripture is a moment well spent. Stay diligent, friend.

MEDITATION MOMENT

As you consider James' character profile, how relatable is James to you? What part(s) of James' life can you identify with personally?

DAY 2

Slavery.

The word dredges up all manner of emotions, virtually all of them negative. We recoil at the idea of slavery in the twenty-first century and assume that it does not happen in our town, in our backyard. How wrong we are.

I have a friend who is front and center in the fight to eradicate modern-day slavery, specifically sex trafficking. Her name is Susan Norris, and she is the founder and executive director of Rescuing Hope[1]. The mission of Rescuing Hope is "to enlighten the public about sex trafficking in America, educate potential victims and first responders, and empower advocates and survivors." Susan is also the author of a powerful fiction book about sex trafficking called *Rescuing Hope*.

Susan works face to face with women and girls who have been rescued from the sex trafficking industry. She and Rescuing Hope provide much-needed aid to these women in the name of Jesus. Some of the survivors with whom Susan works call her "Mama Susan," and one stated that Susan helped her get from where she was (newly rescued from being trafficked) to where she needed to be. Susan's heart is for the survivor not only to be rescued from the horrors of sex trafficking, but also to thrive as a strong, healthy woman or girl who is worthy of respect and true love.

Susan is a hero to many people, both survivors and those of us who have never experienced the horrors of being trafficked.

Today in our study time, we will hear our mentor James willingly proclaim himself to be a slave to Jesus Christ. Please turn with me to **James 1:1**, read it carefully, then write the entire verse below.

Now, go back and circle the word *servant*, *slave*, or *bondservant*. If you are artsy, draw a set of handcuffs over the word. This is the word on which we will camp today.

Most translations and paraphrases of the Bible use the word *servant*, but a few use either *slave* or *bondservant*. Specifically, the Holman Christian Standard Bible and The Message use the word *slave*, while the New American Standard Bible and the New King James Version use *bondservant*.

The original Greek word used in this verse is *doulos* and lends the idea of a slave or a person who was bought by one who would be his or her master. The sole purpose of a *doulos* was to serve the master, and in becoming the property of the master, the bondslave gave up all individual rights.

For many bondservants, this arrangement was a blessing. Most Jewish people viewed their slaves as part of the family and treated them much like a natural or adopted child. They were protected by Jewish law, and many slaves were entrusted with essential responsibilities by their master.

Let's look at a few other places in Scripture where the word *doulos* occurs so we can gain clarity regarding the meaning of the word. Beneath each reference, note who was speaking and in what context the word *doulos* was used.

Matthew 24:45–47

Acts 4:29

Romans 1:1

2 Corinthians 4:5

As you can see, the Apostle Paul used this word quite generously throughout his writing, even calling himself a bondservant or slave. James, as well, wastes no words or time in telling his readers that he is a bondservant of God. He wanted his readers to know that his allegiance was to Christ.

Interestingly, the word used in James 1:1 for Lord is *kyrios*. Can you guess what it means? It means not only Lord but also master. James was telling his readers that Jesus was his master, and he was Jesus' slave or servant.

Let's look at one more place where Paul used the word *slave* or *bondservant*. Read **Philippians 2:5–11** and explain, in the space below and in your own words, how Paul used *doulos*. Take your time. Do not allow familiarity with the passage to rob you of seeing the beauty in it.

Jesus became a slave or bondservant. What a thought! The One who was there at creation, the One who was part of the triune Godhead, a slave? Jesus allowed Himself to be wrapped in human flesh, born to a poor peasant girl, to be mocked, beaten, and crucified because God desired a relationship with you and me.

If you are a follower of Jesus Christ, you, too, are a bondservant or slave. When you and I ask Jesus to come into our hearts, forgive us of our sins that nailed Him to the cross, and invite Him to live His life through us, we are telling Him that we willingly lay down our right to be our own master and lord. In that moment He becomes our Master and Lord, and we become like James, a servant.

He must increase, but I must decrease. John 3:30

MEDITATION MOMENT:

Perhaps you have never asked Jesus to be the Lord and the Master of your life. You have tried to do life your way, and it never seems to work. You have an emptiness in your soul that you have been attempting to fill with many things, but it remains empty. May I gently suggest that you try Jesus as the filler of that empty hole?

No human breathing earth's air was perfect and holy and good enough to be in a relationship with God. (Romans 3:23)

Because of our utter inability to be good enough to be in a relationship with God, the consequence was spiritual and eternal death. BUT GOD. I love those words. But God made a way through Jesus. (Romans 6:23)

Jesus, the perfect Son of God, came to earth to die in your place. He didn't require you to clean up your act first. He died for you while you were still knee deep in your sin. (Romans 5:8)

If you can recognize your need to restore your relationship with God, all you have to do is believe and ask! Believe that Jesus died in your place. Believe that His death and blood pay the debt for every sin you have ever, and will ever, commit. Ask Him to come into your heart and live His life through you. Ask Him to fill the emptiness of soul that you feel. He will do it. (Romans 10:9–10, 13)

Jesus never turns away a sincere person who wants to be His bondservant and part of the family of God. He will never leave you. He will never decide that you are not worth His time or blood. Jesus is yours, and you are His eternally.

If you have asked Jesus into your heart while reading this lesson, the next step is to tell someone about your decision. Tell a pastor or a Christian friend, someone who can encourage and guide you in your new walk with Christ.

Welcome to the family—the family of God!

DAY 3

When I was growing up in the southern United States, one of the joys of summer was picking dandelions and blowing away the floaty pappus on top. While it was great fun for us, I'm sure my dad was not so thrilled about the whole game as he envisioned every one of those little umbrellas becoming a weed in his beautiful yard.

Dandelions, a weed to most gardeners, are very hard to remove from the lawn once they set up housekeeping because the roots of dandelions can grow as deep as 15 feet. Once those fuzzy heads disperse from the stem, they can travel long distances when propelled by a strong wind, merely because they are so light and airy.

Dandelions do have a few redeeming qualities, although very few. They keep the soil in which they take root aerated, and they encourage minerals and other nutrients that reside deep within the ground to move closer to the surface.

Today in our study time, we will examine **James 1:1** again and find that something more than dandelion floaties was dispersed long ago. Please turn to this passage, read it, then write the portion of the verse that has a similar word to *scatter* in it.

If you wrote the last part of the verse that includes the word *scattered*, *dispersion*, *dispersed*, etc. in it, you are correct.

That's a bit of a cryptic greeting. Who in the world is the recipient of this letter? To figure that out, we must have a history lesson concerning two dispersions, or scatterings, detailed in Scripture. Begin by reading the following verses and answering the questions accompanying them.

Matthew 1:2 – List the genealogy detailed in this verse.

Genesis 49:28 – This verse tells us more about Judah and his brothers from Matthew 1:2. Ultimately they became known as what?

Upon David's son Solomon's death in 931 B.C., the 12 tribes, also known as Israel, split into two kingdoms (1 Kings 12). Israel occupied the Northern Kingdom of the land and consisted of the ten tribes geographically located in the north. The Southern Kingdom became Judah and was made up of the two remaining tribes. God's chosen people were split into two kingdoms, and this remained the state of things for over 200 years.

In 722 B.C. and 586 B.C., something happened that forever changed the chosen people of God. Look up **2 Kings 17:6** and **2 Kings 25:1 and 11**, and note what happened to each kingdom.

Here we find the details of the first dispersion of the Jewish people.

This dispersion was prophesied hundreds of years earlier. Take a look at **Deuteronomy 4:25–27** and note in your own words what God told the Israelites.

In 538 B.C. Cyrus, King of Persia, who had overthrown King Nebuchadnezzar, issued a proclamation giving the Jews in Babylon the right to return to the land of their ancestors. Eventually, many returned to the land of Israel.

Now, let's take a look at the second scattering of God's people, and for this, we will turn to the New Testament.

Christ's mission on earth was to bring salvation to the lost. He did this from a "home base" of Jerusalem and the area of Galilee. The Jewish religious elite, known as the Pharisees and the Sadducees, did not take kindly to the message of salvation offered by Jesus, and they schemed to find a way to kill Jesus. Ultimately, He was crucified on a Roman cross, and the religious leaders were sure they had adequately dealt with this issue of Jesus and His followers.

Ah, but God had a plan. After Jesus' death on the cross, one preacher of the gospel, in particular, raised the ire of the religious elite in Jerusalem. Scan **Acts 7** and note the identity of that preacher and his underlying message.

Which of the Pharisees is mentioned in **Acts 7:58** and **Acts 8:1**?

What took place in **Acts 8:1** as a result of the persecution against the church in Saul's/Paul's day?

The first scattering or dispersion affected the Jews, while the second scattering affected Jewish and Gentile Christians.

In any scattering, there is upheaval, disruption, and loss of precious things. Both biblical dispersions removed people from homes, family, native lands, jobs, and friends. While it must have been painful and challenging at the time, God had a plan: a plan to restore and rebuild the kingdom of Israel. He also had a plan to enlarge His family by extending the opportunity for salvation to all people.

What about you? Do you feel like you have been scattered like a dandelion? Have there been disruption and upheaval in your family, your job, your finances, or your personal life? Has trial or tragedy caused you to feel like a dry dandelion head being hurled by the wind to some unknown destination?

May I give you some good news?

Your scattering did not happen outside of the knowledge and permission of God! Although it may feel like God has forsaken you, He has a plan (Jeremiah 29:11) and a purpose for the scattering He is allowing in your life. He is Sovereign, friend. He sees the big picture, while you and I can see only a portion of the picture in which we currently reside.

Will you trust Him? His heart is for YOU, for your good, and for the growing of your faith.

MEDITATION MOMENT:

Charles H. Spurgeon preached a sermon entitled "A Happy Christian." One sentence from that sermon birthed a quote that was made famous in a song written by Babbie Mason and Eddie Cardwell. Here is the line from Spurgeon's message:

> "The worldling blesses God while he gives him plenty, but the Christian blesses him when he smites him: he believes him to be too wise to err and too good to be unkind; he trusts him where he cannot trace him, looks up to him in the darkest hour, and believes that all is well."[2]

What follows is the quote, often incorrectly attributed to Spurgeon according to Spurgeon.org. I invite you to allow the Lord to speak into your heart from these two quotes.

"God is too wise to be mistaken. God is too good to be unkind. So when you don't understand, When you don't see His plan, When you can't trace His hand, Trust His heart."[3]

[2] Spurgeon, Charles Haddon. Accessed November 7, 2019. https://www.spurgeon.org/resource-library/sermons/a-happy-christian#flipbook/.

[3] Lyrics.com, STANDS4 LLC, 2019. "Trust His Heart Lyrics." Accessed November 7, 2019. https://www.lyrics.com/lyric/5061801/Babbie+Mason.

DAY 4

Charles was a 38-year-old attorney practicing in the nation's capital. He was twice married and had three children from his first marriage. He was a regular guy just trying to make a life and a living for his family...or so it seemed.

In the late 1960s, Charles hit the radar of the most powerful man in the United States. That man later would write these words about Charles, "His instinct for the political jugular and his ability to get things done made him a lightning rod for my own frustrations."[4]

Those around him soon recognized that Charles Colson had little in the way of conscience and was willing to do whatever it took to help the President of the United States, Richard Milhouse Nixon, in his bid for re-election. Colson hired a CIA operative named Howard Hunt to spy on the political opponents of the president. These actions by Colson, along with similar illegalities by others, would become part of Watergate, one of the biggest scandals ever to hit Washington, DC.

Eventually the house of cards that Nixon, Colson, Hunt, H.A. Halderman, G. Gordon Liddy, and John Ehrlichman built came tumbling down. In June of 1972 five men were arrested while attempting to plant bugs at the Democratic National Convention headquarters at The Watergate, a hotel and office building in Washington, DC. Trials took place and men were convicted, but President Nixon seemed to have escaped unscathed.

Then in July of 1973, when Nixon refused to turn over secret tapes to Senate investigators, subpoenas were issued, and the Supreme Court ordered Nixon to turn over the tapes. The recordings were never handed over, but the White House released edited transcripts from them which placed Nixon squarely in the middle of Watergate. One year later, Nixon would be impeached and leave Washington in disgrace over his part in the Watergate scandal.

Charles Colson paid a $5,000 fine and served seven months in prison after he pled guilty to obstruction of justice in the case of Daniel Ellsberg, a former consultant to the National Security Council. Ellsberg had previously leaked a document known as the *Pentagon Papers*, which was a secret history of the Vietnam War. Colson intended to decimate Ellsberg's reputation and credibility as a consultant.

[4] Nixon, Richard M., *RN: The Memoirs of Richard Nixon* (New York: Simon & Schuster, Inc., 1978), 496.

To an outside observer, it seemed that Colson had hit bottom, but God had another plan.

Because of a friend's witness, Charles Colson came to know Jesus Christ as his Lord and Savior before he went to prison. Tom Phillips, president of Raytheon Company, had recently accepted Christ, and in desperation, Colson went to the Phillips' home one night, wanting to know more about what had changed Tom's life. While he was there, Phillips read a portion of C.S. Lewis' powerful book entitled *Mere Christianity* to Colson. The excerpt was about the sin of pride, and Colson left the Phillips' home in deep conviction. In his car, he asked Jesus to come into his heart.

Colson went to prison but came out a few months later with a calling to minister to those who are incarcerated. That calling led him to found Prison Fellowship in 1976. Today, Colson's vision has become "the nation's largest Christian nonprofit serving prisoners, former prisoners, and their families, and a leading advocate for criminal justice reform."[5]

Prisoners around the globe have benefitted from Colson's calling, but what if Colson had allowed himself to become paralyzed by Satan's shame game? What if Colson had bought into Satan's lie that he was a convict and would always be a convict? What if Colson had decided that God surely would never be able to use him because of his past?

What if Colson had allowed his past to speak as a prophecy over his future?

Today I want us to step back and pick up a few verses we read in Day 1. The sentences may have seemed inconsequential to you at first reading, but let's reread it. Please read **John 7:1-5** and answer the following questions.

Where does this scene take place?

Jesus would have been right at home in the Galilee region. This northern area of Israel was home to Him. He had grown up there, and these Galileans were His people…or maybe not.

Who does John tell us speaks to Jesus in the passage?

What do His brothers tell him to do?

Judea was the southern region of the land of Israel and Jerusalem; the city of the Jewish people was there. It seems like reasonable advice.

Verse 5 is incriminating. What does it say about Jesus' brothers and what their tone of voice might have been as they spoke to their Brother?

At the risk of being redundant, our study is of the Book of James and was likely written by which of Jesus' brothers?

Stunning, isn't it? Somewhere along the way, James had gone from facetiousness to faithfulness, from being a doubter to a believer. Does it make you wonder if James was the only brother to do an about-face?

FOR FURTHER STUDY

Find any of the names of Jesus' other siblings that are listed in Scripture. Then, do a study to see if any of them came to believe in their big Brother as Lord and Savior.

What if James had allowed his past to speak as prophecy over his future?

There are countless examples of God taking people who had made a colossal mess and using them mightily in His kingdom. Let's take a look at one more example from Scripture.

Choose one of the passages listed below, read it, then write a brief synopsis of the story of grace detailed in it by answering the following questions:

- **Exodus 3:11–15** and **Exodus 14:19–31**
- **Joshua 2:1, 8–11** and **Joshua 6:22–25**
- **Luke 22:54–62** and **Acts 4:5–12**

Who is the story about?

What unfaithfulness/sin was involved?

When and where did it happen (if detailed in the Scripture)?

How did God use the person in spite of their past?

How do these stories of grace speak to you? Do you sense God calling you to a task in His kingdom, but do not feel qualified because of your past sin?

You, my friend, are not the one person who has sinned so grievously that God cannot use you. Whatever happened in your past does not have to speak as a prophecy over your future. Sure, there may be consequences for the sin you committed, but God has promised to forgive, clean you up, and use you for His glory. Your past only has the power over you that you allow it to have, so step out, say "yes" to God's calling, and watch Him do marvelous things in and through you. You, dear one, are His masterpiece.

MEDITATION MOMENT:

Friend, only you and God know how today's lesson impacted you. Would you take some time to journal about it in this space? Just you and Jesus. He loves you so!

DAY 5

We are friends, right?

Well, friend, I need you to know that today's lesson is not one I slung onto the page without a great deal of prayer and seeking the heart of Jesus. Yesterday we delved into the issue of our pasts and how they do not have to speak as a prophecy over our todays or our tomorrows. I pray it was profound and life-changing for those who struggle with Satan's voice ever in their ear whispering like negative Ned, "You will never____________ because ________________."

Today we are going to an equally profound place with Christ, a place I hope will offer clarity and freedom to many. Shall we go?

Several months ago, while I was working in my office, a message popped into my Messenger inbox from a dear friend. I could hear the distress in her tone as I read her message. She is a rock-solid believer in Christ who has a beautiful testimony of multiple instances of His faithfulness in her life. Like you and me, she is not perfect. She has walked some difficult roads and made some decisions in her past that the Bible calls sin, yet grace and peace overshadow her life.

My friend was in a struggle when she messaged me. A situation had arisen within her sphere of influence that would necessitate her taking a stand against a particular issue, a stand that would likely not be popular. She knew how she felt about the circumstance, yet Satan was doing what he does best—whispering condemnation into her ear. He was using his tired old line that goes like this: "Who are you to speak in opposition to this issue? You have __________________ in your past? You did ____________________."

Sound familiar?

Although we will not open the Book of James today, I am convinced, to the marrow of my bones, that James would approve of our excursion into the writings of his fellow apostle, John. He would want us to move forward in our study of his book with a healthy view of sin and the Christian life.

Let's go back to basics. Please read the following scriptures and answer the questions that accompany them in the space provided.

Billions of people have lived on this earth since the time of Creation. How many of them have been disobedient to God, or sinned, according to **Romans 3:23**?

What did Jesus say about sin in **John 8:34**?

Well, stink! Let's close up shop and go home right now. Everyone sins, so that makes us all slaves to sin, right? Wrong! Don't pack your bags yet! Keep going.

Read **1 John 3:4–10** carefully, then make a list of everything this passage tells us about sin.

We will focus today on two words in this passage. I believe this will help us in our understanding of sin and how, in spite of our past sin, we can stand on solid footing when we speak against unbiblical practices in our culture.

Let's look back at **verse 4**. My ESV translation offers the verse in this way:

> *Everyone who makes a practice of sinning also practices lawlessness; sin is lawlessness.*

Consider the phrase, "makes a practice of." Various translations use words like commits sin or sins. The idea that John is conveying here is that those who habitually repeat the same sin over and over with little remorse practice lawlessness or unrighteousness.

While all sin sent Jesus to the cross, there is a difference in persons whose hearts are grieved by their sin and persons who make sin the habit and practice of their life. There is a heart difference between these two people, and God discerns it.

1 John 3:6 elaborates further. Write the verse below.

Let's now take a look at the word *abide*. Your translation may say "lives in Him," "remains in Him," or "continues to live in Him." You get the idea, I think. No one who makes a conscious decision to walk and live in relationship with Jesus can be comfortable living in sin. I know this one. I tried it for many years in my 20s.

After receiving Jesus as my Savior at 15, I turned my back on Him in my 20s, living in ways that I knew were sinful, yet thinking that...well, I have no idea what I was thinking! I might have been the poster child for Psalm 50:21. Take a look at it and feel the full weight of what God is saying through the psalmist. Paraphrase this verse below, and if it steps on your toes, personalize it to yourself. I'll give you an example.

Leah, you lived in ways that you knew were sinful and not fitting for a child of God. I was silent for a while, and you thought I was like you, turning My head at sin. No, ma'am, I do not turn My head at sin. I call it what it is and call you out over it.

Now, it is your turn to paraphrase **Psalm 50:21**.

As we think back to 1 John 3:4–10, I hope you can see that this entire passage speaks to one of the key ways to distinguish God's kids from Satan's kids. Everything hinges on the issues of practicing sin and abiding in Jesus.

Abiders do not practice sin. Practicers of sin do not abide in Christ. It is that simple.

If you have sinned and asked God to forgive you, if you have turned away from that sin and are walking daily with Jesus, your sin is forgiven and forgotten by God. He never brings it back up. He looks at you through the blood of Jesus and does not see that sin. He will never condemn you for it.

So, if you are like my friend and in a place where you need to speak out against something unholy and unrighteous, know that you can do so without condemnation from God. You must do it lovingly and with the heart of Jesus, allowing the Holy Spirit to work through you. When Satan tries to convince you that you have no right to speak because of your past, tell him that Jesus' blood covers your past and that you are clean before God.

MEDITATION MOMENT:

Let's finish today by reading Psalm 51.

Here we find David saying a hearty "Amen" to what John is telling us. King David wrote this after Nathan confronted him about his sin with Bathsheba. Recall that David had kept the secret of his sexual sin and the murder of Bathsheba's husband, Uriah, for a year. Perhaps he thought no one knew and that he would get away with it.

God knew, and God was not turning a blind eye to David's practice of sin, a practice that was eating him alive. Sin is like that, you know. It is ravenous and can never be satisfied.

If you are practicing sin, I want to encourage you that there is peace to be had if you will confess it and turn from it. You can cry out together with David, *Have mercy on me, O God, according to your steadfast love; according to your abundant mercy blot out my transgressions* (Psalm 51:1). He will do it, and you will know peace. Journal in the space below about anything the Holy Spirit brings to your mind.

WEEK TWO

Count It All Joy

My first thought was to title this week of study, "Trials and Temptations." Granted, we will talk about both trials and temptations, but that title just sent me into full-on Eeyore. I wanted to walk around with my head hung low singing along with the *Hee Haw* bunch:

> Gloom, despair, and agony on me.
> Deep dark depression, excessive misery.
> If it weren't for bad luck, I'd have no luck at all.
> Gloom, despair, and agony on me.[6]

No way! I could not do it.

While trials and temptation are part of the human experience, we who pronounce the name of Christ over our lives have good news to share. This week in our study, James comes alongside us as our mentor and reminds us that trials have a purpose. The goal of our trials is to bring forth Christ-like characteristics that shout to a world seeking a reason to follow Jesus.

The world does not take much notice when following Christ is easy for the Christian. What gobsmacks the unsaved world is when a Christian walks through the middle of a trial with peace, joy, and patience. The person without Christ has no experience with that, but it draws them toward Christ like a moth to a bright light.

James minces no words this week. He shoots straight about the fact that trials and tests will be part of the life of a Christian. Yet, he is full of hope and encouragement. I love his words in the verse I have chosen as our memory verse for the week. Please write **James 1:5** in the space below and claim its promise for your life.

---

[6] Clark, Roy, Gordie Tapp, Grandpa Jones, Archie Campbell, "Gloom, Despair, and Agony," *Hee Haw*, written by Bernie Brillstein, Frank Peppiatt, and John Aylesworth, directed by Bill Davis and Bob Boatman, CBS, The Nashville Network, 1969-1997.

Recipe

Cuban Black Beans

Last week I shared a recipe for Creamy Chicken Enchiladas with you, and I hope you fell in love with it. This week I am sharing a recipe for Cuban Black Beans that I make when we have the enchiladas.

I found this recipe by Carol Bullock on Food.com many years ago and have adapted it to our taste buds. It is easy to make and so incredibly delicious, especially when served on a bed of rice. I hope you like it too.

RECIPE

Frijoles Negros (Cuban Black Beans)

- 2 10 oz. cans **black beans** with liquid
- 1 **medium onion**, chopped
- 1 **green pepper**, chopped
- 1 **garlic clove**, minced
- 1 teaspoon **cumin powder**
- ½ teaspoon **oregano**
- ½ teaspoon **salt**
- 1 tablespoon **red wine vinegar**

Fry the onion and pepper in a little oil until onions are translucent. Add the garlic and sauté 1 minute.

Add the beans with the liquid and the spices. Simmer about 30 minutes, then add the vinegar just before serving.

DAY 1

In the space of 48 hours, news came to me that a friend's husband had been arrested, another friend and her husband had separated, and a third friend's husband had taken his own life right in front of her. It was almost more than my heart could bear. All this happened as I was beginning to write this week of study.

Count it all joy.

Seriously, James? All of it? Joy? Why not count it all pain? Perhaps count it all tragedy? Or even count it all "that's just the way life is"? But, count it all joy? Are you sure?

Our friend James had not lived in a happy bubble when he wrote these words. No, ma'am, he had seen some suffering in his day. For him to command his readers to count it all joy when trials meet up with us on the road of life, offers us an opportunity to delve into why he could and would say such a thing.

Today our focus will land on **James 1:2**. Would you write this verse in the space below?

Some translations may say, "Consider it all joy" or "Consider it pure joy." No matter how the verse begins, this one causes many Christians to scratch their heads in confusion.

Let's start with making sure we understand what the word *joy* means. The Greek word is *chara*, and it means what you might think it means—joy or gladness. What I do not believe it means is goofy, giddy silliness. Instead, it is an inner heart joy that is present because of our relationship with Jesus Christ. It is a sense of joy that comes from understanding the sovereignty of God.

The kind of joy that James was commanding believers to have is not a joy because you FEEL joyful. Instead, it is a joy of the will—a joy that comes because you are a follower of Christ and have decided to take Him up on His promise of joy from the Holy Spirit.

Shall we look at an instance in Scripture where people experienced this kind of joy amid trials and suffering? Please read **Acts 5:17–42** and answer the following questions:

What trials experienced by Peter and the apostles does James tell us about in this passage?

Why were they in prison? (Hint: You will need to look back at Acts 5:12–16.)

What miracle took place in this passage?

What did the angel of the Lord tell the apostles to do when they left the prison?

Put yourself in the sandals of the apostles. How difficult would it have been to obey the angel of the Lord, given that you had been thrown in prison because you were preaching about Jesus?

When the high priest questioned them about why they were teaching once again, what did they say?

Do not miss that the word *obey* is used twice in the response the apostles gave the high priest. Even in the face of severe punishment, the apostles were obedient to the command of Christ to go into all the world and preach the gospel.

After they were beaten, they were told not to continue to preach and were released. In **verse 41**, what was the first response of the apostles?

Obedience to God keeps us in a right relationship with Him and brings joy to our hearts.

Before we close for the day, let's peek at one more person who knew joy because of His obedience. Turn to **Hebrews 12:1–3** and note who was obedient to God.

What do you think the writer of Hebrews meant when he said about Jesus, *for the joy that was set before Him* (**vs 2**)?

No human has ever endured the kind of pain and abandonment experienced by Christ on the cross. He did it for you and me so we could have an example of obedience bringing joy to follow as we tread earth's dusty sod.

In our study tomorrow, we find out the ultimate reason James calls us *to count it all joy…when [we] meet trials of various kinds* (James 1:2).

MEDITATION MOMENT:

Do you struggle with joy? Is there an area of your life where disobedience is clogging up the joy stream that runs from the Holy Spirit to your heart? Perhaps it is time to have a chat with your heavenly Father about it. Feel free to journal about it here.

DAY 2

Two frogs fell into a deep cream bowl,
One was an optimistic soul;
But the other took the gloomy view,
"We shall drown," he cried, without more ado.
So with a last despairing cry,
He flung up his legs and said, "Good-bye."
Quoth the other frog with a merry grin,
"I can't get out, but I won't give in.
I'll just swim round till my strength is spent,
Then will I die the more content."
Bravely he swam till it would seem
His struggles began to churn the cream.
On the top of the butter at last he stopped,
And out of the bowl, he gaily hopped.
What of the moral? 'Tis easily found:
If you can't hop out, keep swimming round.[7]

This funny little poem perfectly illustrates the verses we will focus on today. Turn to **James 1:3–4** and write them in the space below.

Yesterday we went headfirst into James 1:2, but in truth, one cannot understand that verse without studying verses 3–4. I left you hanging a bit yesterday, but we will put a bow on this whole "count it all joy" thing by the end of our time together today.

First, I want to summarize these verses in a way that makes sense to me. I hope it does to you, as well.

Trials test our faith.

The testing of our faith produces steadfastness, perseverance, or patience.

[7] Swindoll, Charles R., *Swindoll's Ultimate Book of Illustrations & Quotes.* (Nashville, TN: Thomas Nelson, 1998), 440-441.

Perseverance produces a more Christ-like, or complete, believer.

Let's visit with someone who experienced cultural changes, abandonment, slavery, and imprisonment, yet he never lost his faith. You may know the story of Joseph like the back of your hand, but I ask you to consider it now with a fresh heart.

Read each of the following scriptures and answer the questions that accompany them.

Genesis 37:2 – Who is mentioned in this verse, and how old is he?

Genesis 37:3–11 – Briefly describe how Joseph's actions set him at odds with his brothers.

Genesis 37:18–36 – What did Joseph's brothers do to him because of their jealousy and hatred?

As if all this were not enough, in Genesis 39 we find Joseph being falsely accused of seducing his boss's wife and thrown in prison. He remained in prison for two years, seemingly forgotten by everyone. After two years he was released and ultimately became the right-hand man to Pharaoh, the ruler of Egypt, at 30 years of age.

You might think that Joseph would be bitter about all that happened to him, but guess what? We have no evidence that bitterness overtook Joseph. None.

Joseph prophesied about a coming famine in Egypt that would last for seven years. Consequently, Pharaoh charged him with the task of storing up food and grain in sufficient quantities to feed all of Egypt during the famine.

The famine eventually drove Joseph's brothers out of Canaan and into Egypt to look for food. Where did they go when they arrived in Egypt? You guessed it:

straight to Pharaoh's right-hand man, Joseph. At first, they did not recognize him. Once they did, they were terrified that he would retaliate for what they did to him all those decades ago. Joseph felt no need to retaliate and was eager to provide enough food to his father's family for them to survive and thrive in Egypt.

There is so much more to Joseph's story, but I want you to fast-forward to a part of Joseph's story that brings me to my knees every time I read it.

Read **Genesis 50:15–21**, paying particular attention to verses 19 and 20.

What was Joseph's attitude toward his brothers?

What do Joseph's words to his brothers tell you about his heart? As best you can tell from this part of the story that God has given us, was Joseph bitter toward his brothers, or was there joy and peace in his heart at being reconnected with his family?

How do you see the sovereignty of God working in Joseph's life?

You see, when James tells believers *to count it all joy…when you meet trials* (vs 1), he is looking through the lens of the sovereignty of God. James understands that we must suffer trials to develop perseverance. He knows that perseverance will ultimately grow our faith and help us to become *complete, lacking in nothing* (vs 4).

James is not encouraging us toward fake joy in the middle of trials. Instead, he wants us to allow the Holy Spirit to work out that fruit of joy in our hearts as we persevere through trials. Joy amid trials is not some pie-in-the-sky ideal. It is something that each of us can experience if we will only allow the Spirit to take control of our hearts and minds.

So, count it all joy, my friend, when you go through trials because God intends to bring you out on the other end as a gleaming representation of Jesus. Remember Joseph and trust that God means it for good.

MEDITATION MOMENT:

Encourage your heart by journaling about a time when you went through a trial, and you experienced God's refining work in your life because of that trial.

DAY 3

I have worked as a pharmacist for many years since graduating from pharmacy school in 1987. But the truth is that I do not find fulfillment or meaning in that profession. So for many years, I have been praying about a new career path.

In 2018 the Lord showed me that new path when He led me to train as a Biblical Life Coach. Satan tried to whisper lies into my heart. "You are too old to start a new career. You will never be able to make any money at that." I knew what I had heard from the Lord, so I moved forward with training and setting up a coaching business.

For those who are not familiar with life coaching, allow me a bit of space to share about it. Life coaching is not counseling, therapy, or even mentoring. A life coach does not give advice or diagnose any physical or emotional problems. Who are ideal life-coaching clients? They are persons who are well adjusted, healthy from an emotional standpoint, functioning well in their family, job, and community. Life-coaching clients know they want and, perhaps, need to make a change or changes in their lives, but need some guidance, structure, and accountability to do so.

A life coach uses the two skills of listening and asking thought-provoking questions of their clients so the clients can think through whatever problems are before them. This process allows the clients to formulate solutions to their problem themselves.

Naively, I thought life coaching would be easy. NOT!!! I am a natural teacher and mentor, both of which use skills of teaching and telling. I am not a natural, powerful question asker, but I am learning.

Today's Scripture passage in James deals with wisdom, something that I have needed tons of in my coaching practice. I need God's wisdom to hear the hearts of my clients and to know the right questions to ask.

Let's see what James will teach us about wisdom. Please turn to **James 1:5–8** and write the verses in the space below.

The Greek word used by James for wisdom is *sophia*. When this word is used in New Testament scriptures, it means practical wisdom used in daily life. This is God-given wisdom and discernment rather than human wisdom. Old timers would have said of a person who did not have this kind of wisdom that "they just don't have good sense."

Honestly, I love verse 5! It is simple, yet so full of promise. If I lack wisdom, which I often do, all I have to do is ask God for it, and He will give it to me. Not only will He provide me with wisdom, but He also will give it generously. I don't know much that is better than that.

There are a couple of caveats, however. I must ask for wisdom, be confident that God will give it to me, and live by it. If I sway back and forth between God's wisdom and my wisdom, Scripture says that I am a double-minded person who is unstable in all my ways. Until I decide to settle into God's wisdom, I cannot assume that God is going to entrust me with His wisdom.

Whoa! This is serious stuff, y'all. God is so holy, righteous, and wise that He is not going to waste His wisdom on people who will not administer it well. So, we are wise to delve into Scripture and learn all we can about wisdom.

Please read the following verses and answer the questions that accompany them.

Often called the wisest man who ever lived, King Solomon knew a bit about wisdom. He knew it because God gave him wisdom, and he also knew it because he had been one of those people who didn't have a lick of sense. Let's visit with him a bit.

In **1 Kings 3:3–12**, we find Solomon in conversation with God through a dream. In verse 5, what did God say to Solomon?

Summarize Solomon's response in **verses 6–9**.

God was pleased by Solomon's request. What things did God commend Solomon for NOT asking for in **verse 11**?

Why do you think God commended Solomon for not asking for these three specific things?

God is a God of abundance, so there is gravy on the top of Solomon's biscuit of blessing. Take a quick look at **verses 13 and 14** and note what God gave Solomon in addition to wisdom. Note, also, the stipulation God placed on Solomon experiencing a long life.

FOR FURTHER STUDY

Read **1 Kings 4:20-34** to learn the specifics of how God answered Solomon's request.

Unfortunately, Solomon did not administer his wisdom well, and eventually, God tore the kingdom away from Solomon. Turn to **1 Kings 11** and read **verses 1–8**. List the acts of Solomon that brought God's judgment on him and his family.

Friends, I have ample evidence from my own life that my wisdom is not very wise. It has put me in a ditch more than once. I want to be filled with God's wisdom for this life—for my marriage, my career, my family, my friends, and so much more. God is generous with His wisdom, but He is also serious about how we administer it.

I want to encourage you to ask God for wisdom today, then have faith that He will give it to you in His way and His timing.

MEDITATION MOMENT:

The book of Proverbs is most often attributed to King Solomon. Choose one or more of the passages below, read it, and ask God to teach you from it.

- **Proverbs 1:1–7**
- **Proverbs 2:1–8**
- **Proverbs 3:5–8**

DAY 4

One of my heroes of the Christian faith is Dietrich Bonhoeffer, the German theologian, pastor, writer, musician, and martyr. Bonhoeffer stood in direct opposition to Hitler and was part of a conspiracy to stop Hitler's extermination of the Jews. He was martyred in a concentration camp, just days before troops liberated the camps in 1945.

I highly recommend the marvelous biography about the life of Deitrich Bonhoeffer written by Eric Metaxas. *Bonhoeffer: Pastor, Prophet, Martyr, Spy* is a fascinating look into the workings of Nazi Germany, and the mind of a man completely sold out to Christ. It is also a frightening story of the slippery slope of apathy that leads to the fall of a nation. America, beware!

In his book entitled *Temptation,* Bonhoeffer offers words that are a perfect opening to our study today:

> In our members, there is a slumbering inclination towards desire which is both sudden and fierce. With irresistible power, desire seizes mastery over the flesh. All at once, a secret, smoldering fire is kindled. The flesh burns and is in flames. It makes no difference whether it is sexual desire or ambition or vanity or desire for revenge or love of fame and power or greed for money....
>
> Joy in God is...extinguished in us, and we seek all our joy in the creature. At this moment, God is quite unreal to us, he loses all reality, and only desire for the creature is real; the only reality is the devil. Satan does not fill us with hatred of God, but with forgetfulness of God.... The lust thus aroused envelops the mind and will of man in deepest darkness. The powers of clear discrimination and of decision are taken from us. [8]

Quite the description of temptation, huh? Let's see what James has to say about temptation. Please turn to **James 1:12–15** and write these verses in the space below.

I will be the first to admit that James' word choices are mighty confusing. Trials, tests, tempt, tempted (three different times). What in the world?

It seems a bit of a hot mess until you dig around and learn about the meaning of the Greek words used in these verses. Let me see if I can help clear it up a bit.

Go back to where you wrote our verses at the beginning of today's study. In verse 12, please circle the word *trial* (or *temptation*) and the phrase *stood the test* (or *been approved*).

The Greek word James uses for trial (or temptation) in verse 12 is *peirasmos*, and it means a trial or a test, putting to the test. It is a generic word that may be ascribed to either God or Satan as the agent. If God is putting someone to the test, the purpose of the test is always to purify the faith of the one enduring the trial. If Satan is the agent, the goal is always to cause the person to fall and fail.

The second Greek word we need to consider is *dokimos*, and it is used to signify one that has remained faithful through trial and, in the end, is approved by God.

So Leah's version of verse 12 might read "Blessed is the man who remains steadfast under trial and temptation, for when he has been faithful to the end, he will be approved by God and receive the crown of life."

Now, go back to our focus verses once again. In verse 13, the word *tempt* or *tempted* is used four times. Please underline each usage or the words that correspond to *tempt* or *tempted*.

The first, second, and fourth times this word, or a form of the word, is used, the Greek word is always *peirazo*. This word carries the meaning of enticing or baiting a hook so that a person falls into sin. There is evil intention behind this action because the person baiting the hook wants the victim to sin so they can prove the "badness" of that person. The same is true in verse 14, when the word *tempted* is used.

In verse 13, we find the third usage of a form of the word *tempt*. The Greek word is the opposite of *peirazo—apeirastos*, which means the person or persons referenced are not capable of being tempted by evil.

So, what James is trying to tell us is that when we are enticed toward sin, when the hook is baited and ready for us to bite, Satan is always the culprit. God is not capable of baiting a hook and enticing His children to sin.

I want us to camp for just a few moments on verse 14. It is almost as if someone had said, one too many times, "I am being tempted by God." James had all he could take.

Picture it. James looks at his audience with fire in his eyes and says something along these lines:

> "Listen here. You have no one to blame for the mess you are in except yourself. You allowed yourself to be lured into the snare of sin because you were not diligent in staying focused on Jesus. Deep in your heart, you desired something that would cause you trouble.
>
> "Don't tell me you didn't! You thought about it and mulled it over in the hidden place of your heart. You wanted it so badly you could taste it. So, when Satan dangled it in front of you, you were already gone in your heart. You fell hook, line, and sinker into that sin, and it will bring forth death. Maybe not physical death, but there will be a death of some kind. Perhaps it is the death of your integrity, your character, your ability to withstand the temptation to take the bait the next time. It might be the death of your self-respect or the death of the intimacy of your relationship with Jesus."

You see, friends, the devil did not make you do it. Whatever the "it" is in each of our lives, Satan did not make us do it. Oh sure, he tossed out the line with the hook on it, but none of us have to take the bait. If we will deal honestly with God concerning whatever pet sin we keep hidden deep in our heart, we will not be able to be lured and enticed by Satan's tired old schemes. God will give us what we need to overcome temptation.

You and I must set boundaries for how much of the territory of our mind and heart we give to Satan. Each of us reaps what we sow. If we sow integrity and purity, we will reap faith and peace, but if we sow deceit and deception, we will reap sin and death. It is an unbreakable spiritual principle.

Ralph Waldo Emerson said it like this: "Sow a thought, and you reap an action; sow an act, and you reap a habit; sow a habit, and you reap a character; sow a character, and you reap a destiny." There is a definite progression from thought to destiny, and this can be applied to godly and ungodly lives and hearts.

What about you, friend? Is there a secret place in your heart, a hidden compartment where you have put up a "Keep Out" sign for Jesus? Oh, please, please, before it is too late, fling wide the door to that space and let the Holy Spirit do some house cleaning. Let Him replace the fear and embarrassment of "what if someone finds out" with the joy and peace that comes from allowing Jesus to wipe that sin away forever.

MEDITATION MOMENT:

In Psalm 107, the psalmist is recounting the faithfulness of God to the children of Israel during their wilderness wanderings. As you recall, Israel repeatedly fell into a cycle of faithfulness to God, apathy toward God, outright unfaithfulness, captivity, repentance, and return to faithfulness. Please read this psalm and take special note of verses 6, 13, 19, and 28. Journal in the space below how the Lord speaks to you as you read of God's tender heart toward His people.

DAY 5

Many years ago, not too long after Greg and I had moved back to our hometown, I received a call from a woman who had also grown up in our hometown. There were several years difference in our ages, which meant we were never close growing up. That should have been my first clue that there was an ulterior motive behind her call. Sometimes I am naive.

She wanted to meet for lunch to "catch up" on what had been going on in our lives. I thought it a bit odd but agreed to meet her anyway. We met at a local restaurant, and after exchanging pleasantries, she launched into a sales pitch for a company she had recently joined.

Y'all, I was so mad I could hardly be civil during the rest of the lunch. I had been deceived and had fallen for it. I'm not sure if I was angrier at the woman for not telling the truth about why she wanted to meet, or myself for falling for it. I managed to be cordial, ended the luncheon as quickly as possible, and left the restaurant.

Deception. I'm pretty sure that no one wakes up one morning and thinks, "Someone needs to deceive me today." Nope! Not a soul in their right mind would welcome deception, yet too often we fall for it just like I fell for the "let's have lunch and catch up" line.

Today we will listen as James gives us a warning about deception. Please write **James 1:16–18** in the space below and circle the word *deceived* or the similar word.

In verse 16, our friend James is not using his sweet, calm voice. He is giving his readers a command, an imperative. He is commanding them not to allow themselves to be deceived or led astray. Can you hear the urgency in his tone?

It is safe to assume that some of James' flock was being deceived and led to believe that their temptations and the consequences that follow are straight from the hand of God. James wants to stop this lie cold.

While we may be confident that God does not tempt us, so often we are deceived by other lies from the enemy. In our time together today, I want us to consider a few deceptions, or lies, to which we might fall victim if we are not careful to stay focused on Jesus and His Word.

Lie #1 (three lies clustered together)

I Must Earn God's Love
I Must Be Perfect
My Performance Determines My Worth

If any of these are true, two questions demand answers. What exactly do I have to do to earn God's love, and when will I know if I have done enough of the right things?

So, friend, how many perfect people do you know? I didn't ask, "How many people do you know who *think* they are perfect?" I asked how many perfect people do you know. Right-o, the same number as me. Zero! None! Nada! So we might as well go ahead and dispel that lie with **Romans 3:10–12**. How do these verses shoot down the perfection lie?

Next in the triad of lies is the one that says I must earn God's love. Really? What does **Hebrews 11:6** tell us pleases God?

Finally, let's look at the third lie in this triad. It says that my performance determines my worth. Hmmm, let's think that through for a moment.

- Moses was a murderer.
- Tamar committed incest with her father-in-law.
- Rahab was a harlot or prostitute.
- David was an adulterer and murderer and liar.
- Matthew was a hated tax collector.
- Peter denied Jesus, not once, but three times.
- Paul killed Christians.

Now, consider how God used each of these people in spite of the sin they committed.

- Moses was God's chosen servant to lead the Israelites to the Promised Land.
- Tamar and Rahab are named in the lineage of Jesus Christ.
- God called David a man after His own heart, and David was the great "several times removed" grandfather of Jesus.
- Matthew was entrusted with writing a gospel account of Jesus' life.
- Peter, bless Peter's heart, was a leader in the early church.
- Paul became one of the greatest evangelists the world has ever known.

Need a bit more reinforcement? Turn to **Ephesians 2:8–9** and note what Paul says is the way into God's family.

Oh, dear one, there is nothing you can DO to make yourself more valuable to God than you are right now. Conversely, there is nothing you can DO to make yourself less valuable to God. God loves you, no matter how you perform.

Lie #2

Because of your past, you will always be like you are now.

Oh, this one is most assuredly a lie from the pit of hell. Satan's desire is to bind us in the chains of our past because he knows it will render us utterly ineffective for the Kingdom of God.

May I declare something over you? Your past does not have to speak as a prophecy over your future. God is more powerful than Satan. Once again, Peter is the absolute poster child for us to consider. He denied Christ three times. Please turn to **Luke 22:54–62** and note below the three verses that detail Peter's denial of Christ. Also, note beside the verse reference Peter's exact words.

Surely, if anyone's past were going to prophesy over their future, it would be one of Jesus' most intimate friends who denied knowing Jesus not one, not two, but three times. The regret that must have threatened to consume Peter! Surely Peter remembered all the times Jesus had blessed him, and now he had become a coward who didn't even acknowledge knowing Jesus. It had to be the most profound agony Peter would ever know.

But, it didn't end there. Please turn to Mark 16. While the story of Jesus' resurrection is told in all of the gospels, only Mark gives us one tiny detail that changes the entire landscape of Peter's life.

In Mark 16, Scripture records the resurrection of Jesus and how it all happened. Three women were the first to witness the empty tomb. When they entered the tomb intending to anoint Christ's body with spices, much to their surprise, *a young man sitting on the right side, dressed in a white robe* (vs 5) greeted them. He told the women that they should not be alarmed. Are you kidding me? Resurrections didn't happen every day. Of course, they were scared.

You seek Jesus of Nazareth, who was crucified. He has risen; He is not here. See the place where they laid him. But go, tell his disciples and Peter that he is going before you to Galilee. There you will see him, just as he told you (vs 6–7).

Go tell His disciples AND PETER. It is almost as if the angel were saying, "Please don't forget to tell Peter." Peter. Three-denial Peter. Be sure and tell him that Jesus is alive.

That tenders my heart so. I cannot imagine what those words must have done for Peter's heart! Jesus is alive. Jesus remembers me and wants me to know He lives.

No! Peter's past did not speak as a prophecy over his future. Neither does your past speak as a prophecy over your future, friend. God specializes in taking your past and making it a trophy of His grace. All He requires is a repentant heart set on following Him.

MEDITATION MOMENT:

What are other lies that Satan has convinced you are true? Would you be bold enough to list them here? Once you do, I would love for you to write these words beside them: "LIE. Grace says it is a lie."

Would you ask the Lord to heal your heart and help you to replace those lies with truth? I'm praying for you.

WEEK THREE

HEART THINGS

Have you heard the quote, "The heart of the matter is the matter of the heart"? It is true.

In our study this week, James is going straight to the matter of the heart. He will address several areas of our lives where we can benefit from regular heart check-ups by the Holy Spirit. I cannot help but believe that James was remembering **Proverbs 4:23** as he put ink to parchment. It would be time well spent and a great foundation for our week of study for you to turn to that verse and write it in the space below.

The writer of Proverbs is adamant about the issue of guarding your heart. He does not put forth this verse as a suggestion, but rather as an imperative—a command. You will notice the same sort of tone in James' writings. Both Solomon and James knew from experience how easy it is to fall headlong into a ditch of sin if we are not attentive to what we allow into our hearts.

Remember the phrase "garbage in, garbage out"? Whatever we allow into our hearts will be the very thing that comes out of our hearts, so let's heed the commands given by James this week and allow the Holy Spirit to stand guard over the entrance to our hearts.

What a perfect segue into our memory verse for the week.

Memory Verse: James 4:17 – *So whoever knows the right thing to do and fails to do it, for him it is sin.*

Pretty convicting, huh? I'll see you in Day 1 of our study after we have a bite of dessert.

Recipe

Leah's Banana Pudding

When I think of a classic Southern dessert, banana pudding comes quickly to mind. It is a rich, creamy confection that includes fruit and dairy, which makes it good for you. Right?

I created this banana pudding recipe by making a few changes to a banana cream pie recipe that I had used previously. It is easy to make and takes very little time, even though you make the pudding from scratch. I promise that it will draw rave reviews from your family and friends.

At our house, we are not fans of meringue, lovingly called calf slobber by my daddy. Instead, our desserts are topped with homemade whipped cream. If you are partial to calf slobber, go right ahead and use it. It won't hurt my feelings one bit. But as for me and my house, we will eat whipped cream.

Either way, I hope your heart is blessed by this banana pudding recipe.

RECIPE — LEAH'S BANANA PUDDING

Pudding:

- 1½ cups **sugar**
- ⅓ cup **cornstarch**
- 4 cups **half and half**
- 8 **egg yolks**
- 6 tablespoons **butter**
- 1 tablespoon **vanilla flavoring**
- 4–6 **bananas**, sliced
- 1 box **vanilla wafers**

Whipped Cream Topping:

- 2 cups **heavy whipping cream**
- ½ cup **sugar**
- ½ teaspoon **vanilla flavoring**

Pudding Instructions: In a medium saucepan mix sugar and cornstarch. Add half and half and egg yolks and whisk until well combined. Bring to boil over medium heat, stirring constantly. Boil for 30 seconds and remove from heat. Stir in butter and vanilla.

Place ½ of pudding in the bottom of 9 x 13 baking dish. Cover with layers of vanilla wafers and bananas. Repeat using the remainder of pudding, bananas, and wafers.

Topping: In a mixing bowl, beat whipping cream at medium-high speed. Gradually add sugar and vanilla, beating until stiff peaks form. Spread whipped cream over the pudding. Serve warm or chilled.

The recipe serves 8-ish people. Calories: Too many to count, so don't worry about it. Just enjoy it!!

DAY 1

Many things in this world do not make sense to me.

- How does an airplane that weighs tons stay in the air?
- Math...of any kind.
- The upside-down economy of God.

The upside-down economy of God is where we will hang out in our study today, and as we do, I want us to look at one facet of it that will help us trust the heart of the Father more.

Let's begin with the verses from James on which we will focus today. Please turn to **James 1:9–11** and write them in the space below.

At first glance, these verses make little sense, yet I believe that as we examine them more closely, we will see the point James was seeking to make.

In the first few verses of James 1, our teacher drives home two points:

God has a purpose for allowing our trials and suffering.

God is more than willing to give us wisdom for life.

Now, James begins to discuss a topic about which his big Brother had a word to say. While James is focusing on "the rich" and "the poor" in these verses, we find he is talking about the condition of the hearts of these two groups of people.

Do you recall what **1 Timothy 6:10** says? Is money itself the problem? Please read it and then note in the space below the message Paul is sending to Timothy.

Again, in **1 Timothy 6:10,** what consequences emerge because of the "love of money?"

In and of itself, money is neutral. It is neither good or evil. Instead, the heart's reaction toward money is what really matters.

Now return to **James 1:9–11**. In these verses, James is not saying that every poor person is exalted, and every rich person is condemned. So, let's brainstorm a bit. What is James' big takeaway in these verses? Write your thoughts below.

I believe what James is telling us is that there is something so much more valuable than money. Often people who have significant sums of money miss Jesus because they believe they are self-sufficient.

Let me state that many wealthy people honor God with their money and trust Him to provide for them. Those who do not may be tempted to trust in their money rather than in God. Even people without great wealth often trust their money more than they trust God!

Money cannot buy anyone a right relationship with God, nor can it buy a ticket into heaven. Money is temporary. One downturn of the stock market, and investors can lose every penny they have. Ultimately, love of money, regardless of the amount of it, will be a person's eternal downfall.

Meanwhile, James was seeking to encourage his readers, many of whom likely had been blessed with a measure of wealth at some point in their lives. He wanted to assure them that in the long run, having Jesus in their hearts was much more beneficial than having shekels in their purse. They would also have the Holy Spirit in their hearts, a one-way ticket to an eternity with God, and an inheritance as a child of God. What a deal!

Let's finish today by looking at one other facet of God's upside down economy. Please turn to **1 Corinthians 1:18–25**. In your own words describe this facet of God's upside-down economy.

How might this passage be an encouragement to you in your walk with Christ?

Let's use our Meditation Moment to wrap up today's study.

MEDITATION MOMENT:

I would like for you to do some heart work today regarding money. I am not trying to get all up in your kitchen. I merely want you to have wealth in its proper place. Would you take some time to talk to God about the following questions and listen to what He wants to tell you?

Do you have debt other than your house payment? If so, write down the dollar amount here.

Do you have money saved for emergencies? Is it at least 3–6 months worth of household expenses?

Do you have money, or does money have you? Do you control your money, or does your money control you?

A person's checkbook or bank statement tells a lot about his or her attitude toward money. What does your checkbook or bank statement say about you?

If someone asked Jesus whether you manage your money well, what would He say?

If Jesus was all you had, would Jesus be enough?

DAY 2

Today we are beginning our study with an episode of "True Confessions," and I'm the one confessing. I have always known that it was not "nice" to show partiality or favoritism, but it was not until I began studying for the writing of this day of our study that I was hit full-force with the sinfulness of partiality.

Why had it never sunk into my head and heart that partiality and showing favoritism is a sin? I think there are a couple of reasons. First, I have never done a word study to see what Scripture says about partiality. (We will take care of that today.) Second, partiality and favoritism are so widespread in our society that we are desensitized to the seriousness of them.

Please take a moment to write **James 2:1–7** in the space below.

Scripture has a lot to say about the topic of partiality, so let's begin with a working definition of the word *partiality* or *partial*. When one shows partiality, they show favoritism, or give preferential treatment, to one person over another.

The idea of partiality is a recurring theme in both the Old Testament and the New Testament scriptures. Read **Deuteronomy 10:17**. Who is referenced in this passage?

What is said about partiality in this verse?

Turn now to **Romans 2:11** and note what this scripture says about partiality.

Having examined what the Bible says about God and partiality, the next question to ask is what Scripture says about partiality in human relationships.

Match the following scriptures with what they say about partiality.

A. 2 Chronicles 19:6–7	The wise person judges impartially.	_____
B. Proverbs 24:23	Priests showed partiality in the law.	_____
C. Malachi 2:9	Discipline church elders fairly.	_____
D. John 7:24	Do not judge by appearance.	_____
E. Ephesians 6:5–9	Judges should not show partiality.	_____
F. 1 Timothy 5:19–21	God judges slaves and masters impartially.	_____

In the space below, please recap what you have learned about partiality in human relationships.

Very often, God uses the outcast, the downcast, the forgotten, or the hated to accomplish His purposes. He was not partial toward the rich, famous, or educated. Please turn to **John 4:1–39** and read the story of the Samaritan woman at the well. How was the impartiality of Jesus evidenced in this story?

The world elevates those who are rich, famous, or successful. God, on the other hand, does not show partiality toward any one group of people. As Christ-followers, neither should we.

One day we will live in a world where there is no partiality or favoritism. Everyone will be equal and equally loved. For the final moments of our study, let's take a glimpse at that world and try to imagine ourselves there. Please turn to **Revelation 7** and read **verses 1–10**. Once you have read these verses, please write **verses 9 and 10** in the space below and circle the words that show God's impartiality toward humanity.

What a day that will be when we, from every nation, tribe, tongue, socio-economic group, skin color, educational level, and any other descriptor you can think of, worship together around the throne of God. There will be no competition for God's attention or love, and no one will feel less than or not enough.

MEDITATION MOMENT:

What emotions or feelings flood your heart when you read **Revelation 7:9–10**? If you have a song that consistently leads your heart to the throne of the Father, consider playing it as you read this powerful passage of Scripture. Journal your thoughts and worship in the space below.

DAY 3

Have you ever been called out by a pack of tissues? Well, I have and let me tell you, it is quite embarrassing. Perhaps I should explain.

One of the jokes between my best friend, Cindy, and me is that when God was giving out mercy, I must have been in the ladies' room. Several years ago, Cindy gave me a gag gift, which revealed that mercy was in low supply in my heart.

The cartoon on the tissues was a well-dressed woman with a look of disdain on her face, holding out a hanky saying, "Oh boo, hoo, hoo. Wipe your nose and get over it."

Up until the past few years, my attitude toward people has generally been one of "you got yourself into it, now deal with it, and quit whining about it."

The verses on which we will focus today are part of the reason I had a heart change several years ago. Please turn with me to **James 2**. Read **verses 8–13**, then write them in the space below.

Today's lesson is one that I long to communicate well because it has the power to impact hearts and lives for eternity. If it were a play, I believe our lesson would be a two-act play. I'll explain what I mean in a moment. Shall we settle in on **verse 13**?

> *For judgment is without mercy to one who has shown no mercy. Mercy triumphs over judgment.*

Mercy Triumphs Over Judgment - Act 1

Act 1 must begin with a definition of mercy, and I am going to offer one that brings me to tears every time I think about it. God looked at you and me and saw the hopeless, helpless state we were in long before we ever breathed earth's

air. His heart was moved, and out of that compassion, He offered a way for us to be in relationship with Him. He gave us what we did not deserve.

Mercy originated with God and flows from God. God is not stingy with mercy. He does not look at me in all my hot mess of sin and say, "Oh boo hoo hoo. Wipe your nose and get over it." Without the mercy of God, there is no getting over sin. Without the mercy of God, I am an eternally lost cause.

God looked at you and me and pitied us. His heart was moved at our misery and our utter inability to rescue ourselves from the consequences of being born into the human race.

When God could have obliterated humanity with one word, He had compassion on us and sent Jesus to provide a way to alleviate our misery and relieve our suffering caused by sin.

The thought of God's heart welling up with pity toward me is probably the most humbling thought I have ever had. Of all the people who have ever breathed earth's air, I deserve God's pity least. God had mercy on me. God had mercy on you.

What is the outcome when God's mercy, love, and grace co-mingle as described by Paul in **Ephesians 2:4–6**?

Mercy Triumphs Over Judgment - Act 2

The answer seems crystal clear about whether you and I are to show mercy to other people. Living a life that reflects Jesus calls us to show mercy to other people, even those who seemingly do not deserve it. In all honesty, who among us does deserve it?

Let me be clear. There will always be situations where tough love is required, where we must hold others accountable for their actions. Yet even in those situations, there is a space for mercy and grace. God's Holy Spirit helps us navigate those times so that we gracefully and lovingly walk that fine line.

Jesus left us a parable that illustrates the absolute necessity of showing mercy. Please read Matthew 18:21–35.

Teaching on forgiveness and mercy, Jesus used the parable of the wicked servant. The story is about an earthly king whose servant owed him money—a lot of money. In today's economy, ten thousand talents would equal approximately six million dollars. I am left wondering why the king would loan a servant so much money, but I digress.

The king decided that all his servants need to pay up or suffer the consequences. The servant who owed ten thousand talents could not pay the king what he owed, so the king ordered the man, his family, and all he owned to be sold to pay his debt.

As anyone would do, the servant begged the king to have patience with him, and he would eventually pay the debt. The chances were good that he would never be able to pay the debt, and the king knew that. However, because the servant requested mercy, the king offered it and forgave the man the debt. Now, that is a king with whom I want to be friends!

One would think that the forgiven servant would be a changed man and be ready to extend mercy to anyone he encountered, but not so. Another servant owed him money, one hundred denarii, an amount equal to about $12,000 in today's economy. It would not come close to paying the debt for which the first servant had been forgiven, but it was still a sizable amount of money.

When the second servant could not pay the first servant the one hundred denarii he owed to him, the first man began choking the debtor, demanding payment.

When the king heard that the first servant refused to show mercy to the second servant, he was so angry he threw the first servant in jail until that man could pay the six million he owed the king.

Friends, this is more than a story about a king, two servants, and a whole lot of dough. Answer the following questions about the parable:

Who does the king in this story represent?

____

____

____

Who does the wicked servant represent?

____

____

____

What do the ten thousand talents represent?

In verse 25, what does the punishment of the wicked servant represent?

When the wicked servant begged for mercy, the king gave it freely. How did God show mercy to us?

Given God's mercy to you and me, how then shall we live? As mercy-full people?

MEDITATION MOMENT:

Is there a person or people in your life to whom you need to show mercy? Would you take some time to talk to Jesus about it all? Use the space below to journal your thoughts.

DAY 4

What method do you use to keep your days, weeks, and months organized, so you do not miss appointments, birthdays, or significant events?

I am a touch-and-feel paper day planner girl. I have used many different brands and styles of day planners throughout my life. After I bought my first iPhone, I decided I would use the electronic calendar included with it. Sure, there were great features, like being able to sync the calendar to my laptop and not having to tote around a physical book, but after a few years, I grew dissatisfied with it and returned to a paper planner.

My planner helps me know what is on my calendar for today, tomorrow, next week, and next month. Sometimes I feel like I would be in the ditch for sure if I did not have that planner because I would not know what I have scheduled for tomorrow or the weeks ahead.

Tomorrow. Our mentor James has something to share with us about tomorrow. I am pretty sure this will be one of those times when James steps on our nail-polished toes, so don't say I didn't warn you.

Please go to **James 4:13–17** and write this passage below. If you have access to a copy of The Message Bible, you might want to use it for this writing because we will use one of the sentences from that paraphrase as our jumping off point.

The sentence I want us to ponder from our set of James verses is **verse 14**, which says, *You don't know the first thing about tomorrow.*

Would you take a moment and write in the space below anything and everything that you know for sure—with 100% certainty—about your life, your people, and your choices tomorrow?

I left a tiny space for you to write in because you cannot say one thing with certainty that tomorrow will bring in your life. Only God sees and abides in our tomorrows.

A reasonable question to ask, then, would be: Is it wrong to make plans for tomorrow? As I write this week of study, I have just returned from the local travel clinic where I received two vaccinations in anticipation of a trip I will be taking to Peru with Compassion International. Is it wrong or sinful for me to plan that trip?

Once again, Brother James is reminding us that our attitude about tomorrow is what is under consideration in these verses. In *The Communicator's Commentary:* James, 1, 2 Peter, Jude,[9] Paul Cedar lists three attitude-related sins that James is calling out in some of his brothers in the faith. Let's examine these to see if we might be guilty of any of them.

The Sin of Presumption

In verse 14 (MSG), James is likely quoting one of his church members when he says, *Today—at the latest, or tomorrow—we're off to such and such a city for the year. We're going to start a business and make a lot of money.*

Whomever this businessman was, he had, in effect, made plans and expected God to bless them. Instead, what does James say his attitude toward his business affairs should have been in **verse 15**?

Was James on solid theological footing by pointing out the pride of making personal plans without asking what God's plans were for them? Let's investigate further.

What does **Proverbs 27:1** add to our study?

Also, look at the parable that Jesus told the crowd in **Luke 12:16–21**. The rich man had been exceedingly blessed and had nowhere to store his crops. He decided to tear down his existing barns and build larger ones. Nothing wrong with that, right? It seems like good business.

Problems begin for him in **verse 19**, and then God gets involved. What was the rich man's ultimate downfall in this passage?

How often do we presume something about our lives and our tomorrows when we have no idea if we will even be breathing earth's air in 24 hours? God calls the person who does that a fool.

The Sin of Boasting

We have all known someone who pridefully boasts about something in their lives: their money, their possessions, their work. No one likes to be around someone who is puffed up with pride and talks about themselves all the time.

In this passage, James is calling out the businessmen as boasters and arrogant. He tells them that such boasting is evil. Why is it evil? Because it sets people up as their own god. They think of themselves more than they think of God.

In **Psalm 34:2**, David tells us about a boasting that is acceptable to God. What is it?

The Sin of Omission

All too often, we believe that the only type of sin about which God is concerned are those sins we "do." James, however, tells us in verse 17 that sometimes it is a sin to "not do" something we know to do. In this case, the businessmen to whom James spoke knew to consult God about their calendars and plans, yet they did not.

There are many examples of the sin of omission in Scripture. I want us to look briefly at one that had far-reaching consequences.

In Exodus 34, God renews His covenant with Moses and the Israelites after the golden calf debacle in chapter 33. What specific words of warning does He give them in **Exodus 34:12**?

Please turn now to **Joshua chapter 9** and read **verses 3–15**. How did Joshua commit a sin of omission?

Scan **2 Samuel 21:1–9**, which takes place approximately 850 years after Joshua made the covenant with the Gibeonites. Note how King Saul broke the covenant Joshua made with the Gibeonites and the consequences that resulted.

Only when we stay close to the Lord through prayer and study of His Word do our words and actions become a beautiful reflection of Jesus in our lives. We must allow the Holy Spirit to do His work of convicting us of sins like we have studied today. Let's take a moment and ask ourselves some hard questions, shall we?

MEDITATION MOMENT:

How often do you make plans without consulting God, and then expect God to bless those plans? Would others say that you boast in yourself or in God? Where in your life have you committed a sin of omission (not doing something you knew to do)?

DAY 5

In J.R.R Tolkien's powerful *Lord of the Rings* series, there is a character named Gollum, a hobbit from the tribe of the Stoors. Gollum is a self-centered, egotistical creature whose original name was Smeagol.

On a fishing trip with his friend, Deagol, they found a ring. Little did Smeagol know how his life was about to change because of the ring. It had such incredible power over him that he would do anything to have it. Ultimately, Gollum became a slave to the power of the ring and abandoned his family and way of life to live in a dark cave with it, calling the ring his "precious." In the end, Gollum was destroyed because of his obsession with, and allegiance to, the ring.[10]

How easy it would be for my name, and your name, to be Gollum unless we are very intentional regarding what we are going to make our "precious" in this life.

As we turn the page on this week of our study in the Book of James, we find James addressing people who have turned money into their "precious." Please turn to **James chapter 5**. Read **verses 1–6**, then write them in the space below.

As with each of our days of study this week, we must keep in mind that James is addressing the attitudes of our heart. He knows that if our attitude is wrong, our actions will very likely be wrong.

The sentence I would like for us to concentrate on today is the last portion of verse 3: *You have laid up treasure in the last days.*

I like the way the New King James Version translates this sentence: *You have heaped up treasure in the last days.* Somehow, the words "heaped up" help with the mental picture that James is seeking to paint. It is a picture of excess being stored up at the expense of other people.

What descriptions does James employ in this passage when he writes about the rich or wealthy and their possessions?

The people to whom James is speaking had built wealth, in part, because they had defrauded the laborers who worked for them. The word picture James uses here is quite dramatic.

Note any descriptions James offers of the plight of the workers in **verses 4 and 6**.

As in other passages where James addresses those with money, he is not condemning the having of money, but rather money having the person. Another passage I would like for us to examine corresponds to the words of James. Please turn to **Matthew 6** and read **verses 19-21 and 24**. In the space below, note any similarities in the Matthew and James passages.

Did you see that earthly treasures, like money, are temporary because they will either corrode or be stolen? Money is not the only thing we tend to store up, however. Let's think in a broader sense for a moment. What are some other things that we "store up" or allow to become our "precious" that have little eternal value when they are placed in a position of prominence over God? I'll give you one example.

- Our bodies—we either become obsessed with body image, or we do not care for our bodies.

Now, it is your turn.

Even if material wealth may not be a treasure for some, God still has gifted us with many treasures, friend. We must be very intentional in our placement of those treasures in our hearts. When we heap up a treasure that becomes a god or idol in our life, we are on the path to corrosion and death. But, when we heap up riches for heaven, we are on the path of life. God blesses us so we can be a blessing to other people. Let's use the treasures we have been gifted with to bless others and glorify God!

MEDITATION MOMENT:

What are some of the treasures with which you have been gifted? List them here and note how you are using them. Do this by placing either an "E" for eternal value or a "C" for corrosion and rust next to the treasure.

If you placed an "E" beside your treasures, know that God is well pleased with you, beloved. Most of us, however, will probably have a few treasures beside which we must place a "C." What actions might you take to turn the "C" into an "E"?

WEEK FOUR

A FAITH THAT WORKS

Faith
Works
Faith *and* Works
Faith *or* Works

We all know that having faith in Jesus Christ as our Lord and Savior, who covered for our sin, is the very thing on which our salvation is based. What we may not be so sure of is how in the world "works" fit into the whole equation.

Depending on the climate of faith in which you were raised, you may have an entirely different view of faith and works than the neighbor sitting next to you in the pew on Sunday. I'm not here to start a war between you and that neighbor. Rather, my goal is to simply allow you to learn what Scripture actually says about faith and works. This week we are going to do a deep dive into these issues of faith and works by hearing from James and from Paul. I believe we will find that faith and works are not mutually exclusive.

This week of our study will be very practical, intensely personal, and an encouragement to you on your faith journey. Thank you for allowing me to be your guide.

Our memory verses this week are from **James 4:7–8a**. Please write them in the space below.

This week's recipe became popular in the 1970s when former Georgia Governor Jimmy Carter's wife, Rosalyn, apparently served it. I wasn't there, but that is what the internet says, and you know you can believe everything the internet says!

Recipe

The Cheddar Pecan Cheese Ring is one of my favorite appetizer recipes because it is the perfect combination of sweet and savory, and it is easy to make. This cheese ring can be served with crackers or toasted French bread. It is also delicious made into a grilled cheese sandwich or as an add-on to a hamburger. I am predicting it will be a hit at your next party.

RECIPE — Cheddar Pecan Cheese Ring

1 pound **sharp cheddar cheese**, grated (Use freshly grated cheese because it holds together better.)

1 cup chopped, toasted **pecans**

1 **small onion**, grated

1 cup **mayonnaise**

¼ teaspoon **black pepper**

Dash **cayenne pepper**

1 cup **strawberry preserves** (Use other berry preserves if you prefer.)

Toast the pecans first so they will have time to cool.

Grate the cheddar cheese and onion into a large bowl. Add pecans, mayo, and peppers. Mix well. Turn the mixture out onto a plate or cheese board and form into a ring. Or, if you have a ring mold on hand, you can use that to chill the cheese ring, then turn it out onto a plate or board for serving.

When ready to serve, place the fruit preserves in the middle of the ring and serve at room temperature. You can make this ahead of time and refrigerate it, but be sure to let it return to room temperature for serving.

The cheese ring keeps well in the fridge for several days.

DAY 1

Several years ago, my husband fulfilled a lifelong dream when he obtained his private pilot's license. Immediately, he began working on getting the certification to become an instrument-rated pilot. For those who are not familiar with aviation terminology, having an instrument rating means the pilot is legal to fly in conditions where he or she cannot visually connect with the earth, such as in fog or clouds.

Recently on a Wednesday, Greg and I flew to Lakeland, Florida, to attend the Sun-n-Fun Airshow. Our flight down to Lakeland was smooth and beautiful. We enjoyed the airshow, especially getting to see the Blue Angels perform. Y'all, the fan-girl in me comes out in a significant way with the Blue Angels. I can hardly be still when I see them. I want to jump and squirm and scream from excitement like a little kid.

I digress.

Greg and I were scheduled to fly back home on Saturday. Unfortunately, the weather did not cooperate, and Greg declared that we would have to drive home since he was not yet instrument-rated to fly in possible conditions that might be along the travel path. While Greg could not help or change the weather, my frustration meter with the situation ran high. This trip was the second time we had flown somewhere and had to drive home due to the weather, and the drive was 9–10 hours long.

The decision was made to let a friend who had driven his car to the airshow fly our plane home, and we would drive his car back to our hometown. Any other time I would have been pumped to be riding in his car, a beautiful red Camaro with black racing stripes. Not this time. We had a ton of luggage and other things we were taking home, and it was all packed and stacked in the Camaro. There was barely room for Greg and me. To say I felt claustrophobic would be an understatement!

Adding to my frustrated, anxious mental state was an allergy attack that had begun the minute we opened the airplane doors in Florida a few days prior. Add to that an angry reaction to a nasal spray that I had used, and I had the perfect storm for an anxiety/panic attack.

I have dealt with anxiety for almost two decades and have taken an anti-anxiety medication for most of that time. The vast majority of the time, my anxiety is well-controlled, but on that trip, I lost control. I began having trouble breathing. The car closed in on me, and I could not hold back the tears. I finally asked Greg to stop and let me walk around, so I could get some fresh air and calm down. It was a rough day, folks.

Very often, when I am stressed, my mouth will engage before my heart. The morning of the panic attack, as I scrolled through Instagram, I saw back-to-back posts from different people that referenced Proverbs 15:1.

A soft answer turns away wrath, but a harsh word stirs up anger.

Then, I clicked over to Facebook, and wouldn't you know it, there was a post using the same verse. I knew God was teaching me something, especially since I had already begun praying about the verses from James on which we will focus today.

"Soft answers, Leah. You are in a difficult situation, and your emotions are running high, but speak kindly."

Thankfully, I heeded the teaching of the Lord, and the day went much more smoothly than it would have had I reacted out of emotion.

Perhaps our friend, James, had heard the voice of the Lord whispering, "Soft answers, James," at some point. Write his words to his Christian brothers and sisters in **James 1:19–21** in the space below.

So much good teaching and information are found in these verses that we could camp here for days, but we will not. Instead, I want us to examine three phrases with two goals in mind.

Goal #1 – Righteousness

Goal #2 – Salvation, or the saving of your soul

Now, those are two big, fancy, Christian-ese words that have simple meanings. Let's break them down before we move ahead.

Righteousness, or as the NIV® translates it, *righteous life*, means living according to the standards of God rather than the standards of our culture and time.

Salvation is easier to understand. It means that a person becomes a child of God by accepting Jesus as Lord and Savior.

Now that we have the end goals in mind, let's look at the three imperatives James uses in verse 19. It is worth noting that when James tells everyone to *let every person be*, he is giving a command to people who are already Christ followers. This assumes that they are currently living this way because of their relationship with Jesus, but James wants to give them a potent reminder of the importance of right living:

Let Every Person Be Quick to Hear

Listening is a gift we can give another person, but unfortunately, we have a deficit of hearing in our world today. Several years ago, I came across a quote that said, "There are two kinds of people: those who are listening, and those who are waiting to speak." (Author Unknown)

Let me tell you, that got personal very fast because I realized that all too often, I am merely waiting to speak in a conversation. James wants us to know the value of listening.

As a life coach, listening is one of the primary tools I use as I work with my clients. This tool was not easy for me to develop, and I have had to work on my listening skills to be a good life coach. In the intake paperwork that I ask my clients to complete, I ask why they desire to be coached. One client was refreshingly honest when she said, "I'm usually the one doing the listening. I am excited about being heard for a change."

What did King Solomon say about listening in **Ecclesiastes 5:1**?

The author of *The New American Commentary Vol. 14: Proverbs, Ecclesiastes, Song of Songs* says the following about this verse:

"Those who draw near simply to listen (i.e., in reverence) do not give themselves any occasion for getting into trouble (as in verses 2–6)." [11]

I love that! Listening keeps us out of trouble!

Let Every Person Be Slow to Speak

I won't go into much discussion on this command because we will camp out next week on the issue of our tongue. Suffice it to say that if we are talking, we cannot be attentive to other people, or to God.

What are the benefits of being slow to speak, detailed in the following verses?

Proverbs 10:19

Proverbs 17:28

Oh my, if I had a dollar for every time my mouth got me into trouble. Can you relate?

Let Every Person Be Slow to Anger

You may be thinking, "Well, Jesus became angry in the temple, so what's the big deal?" Read on, dear friend. The rest of the verse talks about the anger of human beings. There is a difference in righteous anger, which Jesus felt, and the anger of humans, which leads to sinful behavior.

Jesus was offended by the sin and greed of the moneychangers against His Father's house. Scripture never says that He was offended by the actions of others against Himself. Think about Judas and his betrayal of Christ. Think about Peter and his denials of Jesus. Nowhere in the Bible do we find Jesus being angry with Judas or Peter.

You and I are wise to examine our anger motives. Are we offended *for*, or offended *by*?

Write **Proverbs 14:29** in the space below.

How this lesson has stepped on my toes! Perhaps your toes are a bit sore as well?

Meditation Moment:

Friend, if you and I want our lives to reflect Jesus, we must take James' commands to heart. Self-control in the area of our listening and our speaking is part of the fruit of the Holy Spirit living in our hearts. I want to be a godly woman who is known for being a good listener and a prudent speaker. Would you like to make that your goal from now on?

Allow me to close today by praying for us.

Lord Jesus, we are people who desire to look like You to a world that desperately needs You. Our hearts grieve at our failure to be good listeners for our friends, family, and those who circle our lives. Please forgive us for the pride in our hearts that causes us to believe it is more important to speak than to listen. Holy Spirit, please help us to be better listeners and slower speakers. Enable us not to be offended by other people, which leads to unrighteous anger. Help us to recall Your example, Lord, and to model Your love toward others. In Jesus' holy name, Amen.

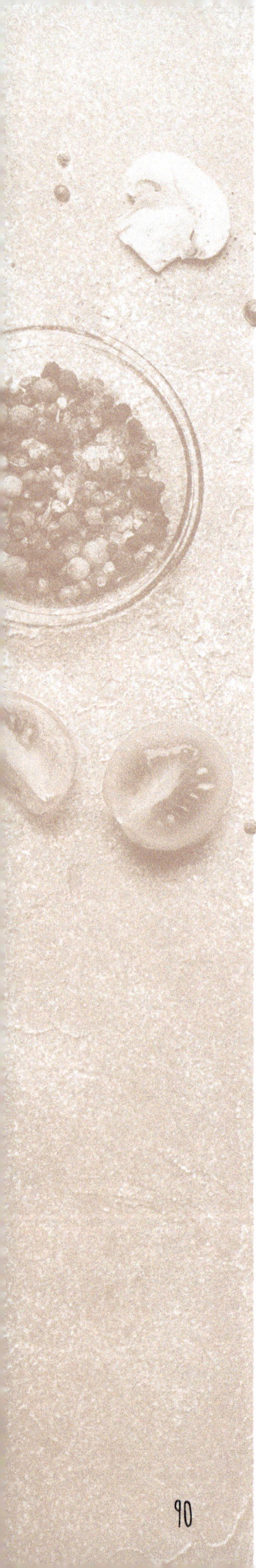

DAY 2

In 2006 and 2010, I was blessed to take what I consider to be trips of a lifetime. Along with a group from my church, I visited the land of Israel. Both trips were fantastic, and I am pretty sure I went around all day slack-jawed and teary-eyed at what we saw.

For several days, Jerusalem was our home base. We saw the Mount of Olives, the Valley of Hinnom, the Church of the Nativity, the Church of the Holy Sepulchre, Golgotha, and the Empty Tomb.

Then, we spent several days in the northern area of Israel known as Galilee, where Jesus was born and ministered. On one of those days, we rode in a boat around the Sea of Galilee, a beautiful 64-square-mile freshwater lake, surrounded by towns and villages.

The Sea of Galilee flows southward along the border of Israel and Jordan, eventually flowing into the Dead Sea, or the Salt Sea. The Dead Sea is the lowest place on earth, situated approximately 1,400 feet below sea level. Its water level continues to decline because of its use by local industries.

Why is this body of water that shares its borders with both Israel and Jordan called the Dead Sea? It is because it has no outlet. Unlike the Sea of Galilee, which has both inlets and an outlet, the Dead Sea has only an inlet. Once the water flows down from the Sea of Galilee and reaches the Dead Sea, it has nowhere to go, so it stagnates. Minerals like magnesium, potassium, bromine, chlorine, and salt build up, and the water becomes unable to support living creatures such as fish and frogs.

These two bodies of water came to my mind as I read today's verses from James, and it occurred to me that there are two kinds of Christians: Sea of Galilee Christians and Dead Sea Christians. Turn to **James 1:22–25**. Read the verses carefully and then write them in the space below.

May I start our study time together by sharing what these verses do NOT say? They do not say that to be saved you have to do specific good works. Let's follow a short rabbit trail to solidify this in our hearts.

How are we saved according to **Ephesians 2:8a**?

From where does salvation come according to **Ephesians 2:8b**?

In **Ephesians 2:9**, we are given a reason why salvation is not a result of anything you and I do. What is that reason?

Finally, according to **Ephesians 2:10**, what were you and I who are in Christ Jesus created for?

Did you notice that the good works for which we were created are applicable only after we are in Christ Jesus? Friend, there is NOTHING you can do to make Him love you more than He does right now. He loved you enough to die for your sins long before you loved Him. That is amazing love!

Okay, back to our James study.

In this passage, we hear James talking to two groups of people:

- Group 1 (Dead Sea Christians): Those who accept the gospel, are saved, but do not live it out
- Group 2 (Sea of Galilee Christians): Those who accept the gospel, are saved, and then live it out

Let's look at Group 1 first. This group of Christians hears the gospel at some point in their lives and responds to it. They say "yes" to Jesus as their Savior, and then go on their merry way, satisfied with "fire insurance." They are likely good people who attend church and maybe even tithe, but their Monday through Saturday lives show little fruit of their salvation.

Like the Dead Sea, they receive salvation but become stagnant because they do not have an outlet for sharing Jesus and His love with other people. Jesus told His followers a parable that has a description of Dead Sea Christians in it.

How does **Matthew 13:22** describe a Dead Sea Christian?

This is the kind of Christian who attends church, bows their head, takes notes, and may even mark their Bible. The only problem is that their Bible never makes a mark on them.

Now, let's turn to Group 2, the Sea of Galilee Christians. These Christians hear the gospel, say yes to Jesus, and then live in such a way that Christ is shown to the world. They have an inlet where they receive the Word; life and faith that grows and blooms; and an outlet, or work, that allows them to share what Jesus has done in their life.

Turn once again to **Matthew 13** and note how this Christian is described in **verse 23**.

FOR FURTHER STUDY:

Read the entire parable of the soils in **Matthew 13:1–23**.

Sea of Galilee Christians are those who are full of joy and peace, even in hard times. They use their gifting and talents to bless other people. They are generous, honest, and have godly character. They are less concerned about getting glory or credit for themselves and more concerned about glorifying the name of Christ. These Christians are willing to let Scripture point out sin in their lives and then let it do a refining work so they will look more like Jesus.

James 1:25 tells us that there is a promise for the Sea of Galilee Christian. What is it?

So, dear reader, which Christian are you: a Sea of Galilee Christian or a Dead Sea Christian? I want to believe that if you have made it to Week 4 of this Bible study you are a Sea of Galilee Christian; however, only you and God know the truth. There are more blessings in being a Sea of Galilee Christian than I could type on this page.

It is all about your heart. You can do and do and do in the name of Jesus and still be a Dead Sea Christian. Only when your heart longs to make Jesus known and you act out of that longing do you become a Sea of Galilee Christian. Gospel in, gospel out.

MEDITATION MOMENT:

I want to encourage you to spend a bit of time with the Holy Spirit and ask Him which kind of Christian you are. Allow Him to point out areas where He needs to do work, as well as areas where you can be encouraged that you are on the right track.

DAY 3

Be the Church!

This exhortation has become quite commonplace in Christian circles in the past few years, but what does it mean?

One meaning of the word "church" describes a building, so it is doubtful that we are being encouraged to be a building.

The biblical meaning of the word "church" describes a group of people who believe in Jesus as the Lord and Savior of their lives and seek to live out the principles of Christ before the world. To "be the Church," a Christ follower should walk, talk, and live like Jesus. Sounds great! How do we do that?

While there are myriad ways that you and I can "be the Church," I had a front-row seat a few months ago that allowed me to observe a group of people who are faithfully and sacrificially living out that calling.

I have the privilege of being a speaker for Compassion International. In that role, I get to share with audiences the work Compassion is doing around the world to rescue children from poverty in the name of Jesus. In April 2019, I was part of a sixteen-person group that traveled to Peru to see the work that Compassion is doing on the ground through the local evangelical church.

Over 200 evangelical churches in Peru are partnering with Compassion to rescue children from poverty, and we were blessed to visit three of them in the city of Trujillo. As a speaker for Compassion, I have a head knowledge of the work that is done in a child development center: children are given medical care and nutrition support, trained in various job skills, taught about Jesus and the Bible, and mentored by volunteers in the church. In the centers that host an infant survival program, expectant mothers may receive prenatal care and assistance with birth. Once their babies are born, mothers "receive training and support to help their babies reach milestones that are critical in early development."[12]

Not until I saw the impact on the life of a child, their family, and their community because a sponsor said "yes" to sponsorship did I truly understand how very much sponsorship matters. I saw children receiving love, care, nourishment, and spiritual training through the Compassion program. I visited with a family who had previously slept five people to one bed who now had bunk beds for their

[12] "Help Babies and Mothers Starting Out." Help Babies and Mothers Survive. Accessed November 7, 2019. https://www.compassion.com/help-mothers-babies-in-poverty.htm.

children because of sponsorship. I heard young men who had been sponsored children now leading worship and seeking to give back because of the impact of the Compassion program on their lives. My jaw dropped and my heart soared when we learned that the program had been so successful in one community that some of the gang leaders were now bringing their children to the church for enrollment in the program.

Y'all, sponsorship through Compassion matters. It matters to the sponsored child, the family, and the community. I saw individuals who were taking the "be the Church" mandate very, very seriously as they lived out their faith before their community.

Please turn with me to **James 2**. Read **verses 14–26**, then write **verses 14–18** in the space below.

At first glance, our buddy, James, seems to be contradicting a foundational tenant of the Christian faith about which Paul spoke extensively. In fact, initially, it appears that he is even contradicting his own teaching from chapter 1. Let's drill down a bit on the issue.

Write out **James 2:14 and 17** in the space below.

Now, write **James 1:17–18**.

In James 1:17–18, Brother James states that every good and perfect gift is from God. Salvation definitely would fit in the "good and perfect gift" category. He goes on to state that it is a gracious act of God, and God alone, to save us by the Word of Truth. Sounds good.

How might **James 2:14 and 17** seem to contradict **James 1:17–18**?

How would you explain this seeming contradiction to a new Christian?

Now, as if the waters were not muddy enough, let's get input from the Apostle Paul. Please choose one of the following passages. Read it and paraphrase what Paul tells us.

- **Galatians 3:6–9**
- **Ephesians 2:8–10**
- **Romans 3:28 and 5:1**
- **Galatians 2:16**

Who is right—Paul or James? Neither? Both? If both are correct, how do you explain their reasoning and logic? Give it a whirl, and then I will share what I believe is the key to reconciling the words of both apostles. Don't peek at my answer until you have pondered it all.

How did you do? I wish we could sit around a table with cups of steaming coffee and talk through this together. Since we cannot, here are my thoughts based on my study.

Have you heard the phrase "context is king"? I believe this is the key to reconciling the words of Paul and James. Think about Bible history for a moment.

To what group of people did Paul primarily minister?

If you said "Gentiles," you are correct. There was always a pesky group of the Jewish religious men who tried very hard to impose the Old Covenant standards of Judaism on new Jewish Christians, and even on Gentiles. So, Paul spent no small amount of time trying to clarify that salvation comes only by faith in Jesus and because of the grace of God. No bodily washings, no repeated offerings to cover sin, no restrictions regarding working on the Sabbath, nothing other than faith in Jesus was necessary for salvation. Paul sought to refute the legalism of his day that surrounded salvation through Christ.

To which group of people did James address his message according to **James 1:1, 16, and 19**?

Yep, Jewish Christians, and probably a good number of Gentile Christians. Brothers. Beloved brothers in the faith who, most likely, had fallen victim to the idea that all you needed was fire insurance from hell. Beyond that, you could live any way you desired.

So, instead of combatting legalism like Paul, James was speaking of "being the Church" and serving as Jesus served out of the overflow of Jesus living in their hearts.

In **James 2:18–25**, James gives examples of people who were saved by their faith and lived out their faith for all the world to see by doing good deeds. He caps off chapter 2 with a final example taken straight from physical science.

According to **verse 26**, what happens to the body when our spirit leaves it?

A body without a spirit is lifeless and useless. So is a faith that is not being lived out. It benefits no one. Dead faith does not inspire anyone to follow Jesus, but a vibrant, living, loving, serving faith is one that draws people to Jesus.

MEDITATION MOMENT:

Carve out 15–20 minutes today to sit before the Lord and ask Him to take the pulse of your faith. Ask Him to show you if it is dead faith, faith that is on a respirator and in need of resuscitation, or a faith that draws other people to Christ. Once you hear from Him, ask Him to give you a desire to live out your faith because Jesus lives in your heart.

DAY 4

Our time together today is going to be very different than usual, but I hope you will like it.

Today we are going to engage with Scripture, beginning with our focus verses, for the purpose of making lists. Oh, how I love a good list!

Almost every day of my life, I have some type of list hanging around because I am a person who functions well with order and a list. It might be a grocery list or a list of the tasks I need to accomplish that day, a list of family birthdays, a list of people to contact about an upcoming event, or a "honey-do" list for my fella. I love lists!

Let's begin today by reading the verses from James that will be our jumping off point. Please turn to **James 3:13–18** and read the passage, then write the verses in the space below.

Our goal today is to build profiles of two kinds of people. In **Proverbs 4:5**, Solomon commands his son to get two things. What are they?

In **Proverbs 4:7**, the king stated that one thing is the most important, or the principle thing. What is that thing?

We are going to read several Scripture passages today in both the Old and New Testaments. Some of the passages will describe God's wisdom and the fruit that comes from it, while other passages will describe worldly wisdom and its corresponding fruit.

Using the following Scripture passages, write the items that fit in each list. I will give you one in each list. There will be repeated words or phrases in each list, so be sure to keep count of how many repetitions you find of each one. Multiple mentions in the Bible offer an idea of the importance God puts on that word or concept.

- **James 3:13–18**
- **Matthew 5:1–10**
- **Proverbs 16:18–23**
- **Proverbs 16:27–30**
- **Galatians 5:19–21**
- **Galatians 5:22–26**

List #1

Words or phrases that describe **godly wisdom** and the **fruit** that comes from it.

- Meekness

List #2

Words or phrases that describe **worldly wisdom** and the **fruit** that comes from it.

- Envy

Now that you have created two lists, please study each list carefully and write any additional general insights you have about them in the spaces below. Perhaps other verses or stories (biblical or extra-biblical) will come to mind when you read the words, or include anything that adds depth or dimension to the lists.

Godly Wisdom and Fruit

Worldly Wisdom and Fruit

Meditation Moment:

As we finish today, we are going to do a bit of heart work with the help of the Holy Spirit. Please take a moment to pray and ask the Lord to reveal to you anything He desires you to see or know from today's work. Here are some ideas to get you started:

- Are you willing to allow the Spirit to do a refining work in your heart today?
- Which descriptors in each list describe your heart and life?
- How are those descriptors impacting your life and the lives of those around you?
- Which descriptors identify an area of your life on which you and the Lord need to work?
- What actions will you take to work on these areas?
- Who might you confide in that would give you support and accountability as you and God work on your heart?
- If a miracle occurred during the night so that the work you have identified had been miraculously accomplished, how would your life be different?

Today's study is all about the heart. If you have identified areas of your life and heart on which you would like to work but are not sure how to get started, or if you know something is not quite right but need help identifying what is missing, you might benefit from life coaching.

Walk in God's wisdom, dear friend. You will never go wrong.

DAY 5

Newsflash!

We live in a world where everyone wants quick fixes and instantaneous results. Here are a few examples from my perusal through the daily news and advertisements:

AT&T – America's Best Network is also the fastest

Amazon Prime – Fast, free, convenient ways to get millions of items

Publix Supermarkets – Easy Grocery Delivery. Shop now. Powered by InstaCart

And my personal favorite.

SKINNY MAGIC! – Fast acting, thermogenic weight loss, increase metabolism, energy booster for men and women, appetite suppressant, sugar cravings.

The truth is that while many things can happen fast, some things take time…a cup of Italian roast coffee brewed in a Chemex, the maturing of a redwood tree.

Such is the case in our relationship with God. It is not a zip-zip, do this, this and this, and you are good to go kind of thing. Instead, it takes time, intentionality, and oh my, humility.

In our time together today, we are going to hear James give us the recipe for an intimate walk with Christ. Please turn to **James 4** and read **verses 1–10** and **17** slowly and thoughtfully.

Now, write **verses 7–8a** and **10** in the space below. These verses will be our focus for today.

In these verses, James gives us four imperatives, or commands, and three promises. Let's take a look at each, but first, see if you can formulate each list below.

Commands/Imperatives

Promises

How did you do?

Let's dive into each imperative, along with its corresponding promise.

Submit to God.

James isn't playing around here. He starts with a biggie: submission. Our culture seizes up when Christians say the "S" word. Why? I believe it is because the culture does not understand the true meaning of biblical submission. The concept our unsaved friends and neighbors likely latch on to is one of being a doormat or a mistreated slave. In reality, nothing could be further from the truth.

Biblical submission to God is all about trust and security. It is about allowing God to direct your life and be responsible for the outcome. When you and I submit to God's authority, direction, and sovereignty in our lives, we do not have to worry about whether we are making the right decisions and choices. He will never direct us down a path that He does not ordain.

Nowhere in Scripture do we find a better example of biblical submission than in **Matthew 26:36–44**. Please read this passage, then answer the following questions:

Who is setting the example of biblical submission?

What is the circumstance or situation that requires submission?

What request did Jesus make of the Father?

What words did He use to show that He was willing to submit to God's plan?

Let's not be so naive as to assume that Jesus liked the plan of God for the salvation of the world. He knew He would experience unspeakable suffering in the coming hours. He knew the Father would turn away from Him. Yet, Jesus submitted to the will of the Father. There was no hint of rebellion in His heart because He trusted His Father completely.

Hebrews 12:2 gives us great insight into how Jesus could submit to God's will in His earthly life. What enabled Him to endure the cross and shame that went with it?

Jesus trusted His Father's sovereignty and wisdom. He had His eyes on the prize at the end of the suffering. Submission comes easier when you trust the One to whom you are submitting.

Resist the devil, and he will flee from you.

I am not going to use much ink on this one. We all understand what it means to say "NO" to temptation and the schemes of the devil. Our problem seems to be understanding that Satan NEVER has good things planned for us. Never.

Let's return to the life of Christ and see how He handled Satan's trickery. Please read **Luke 4:1–13** and answer the following questions.

List the three temptations of Jesus by Satan in the space below.

Temptation #1

Temptation #2

Temptation #3

Now, beneath each temptation list the corresponding response by Jesus and note where it is found in Scripture. He quoted the response. (Note: You may need to use the margin references to find the Scriptural address of His responses.)

Finally, note what happened in **verse 13** as a result of Jesus resisting the devil by using God's Word.

I have to wonder if James had this very incident in mind when he wrote, *resist the devil, and he will flee from you.*

Draw near to God, and he will draw near to you.

Developing an intimate relationship with another person or with God always involves two-way communication. We communicate with God when we talk to Him *and* when we listen for His voice.

God communicates with us primarily through Scripture. The Holy Spirit teaches us God's commands and what pleases His heart so we can live in ways that allow us to draw near to Him. God also communicates through nature, music, art, other people, and so much more.

God is always listening to His children, but the question is, are His children always listening to Him? Drawing near to God and having Him draw near to us requires intentionality and discipline. How are you doing at drawing near to God?

Humble yourselves in the sight of the Lord, and he shall lift you up.

Go low before the Lord! There is both beauty and benefit in humility. Wisdom and wonder flow when we come humbly before God and admit our utter need of Him. Acknowledging our need for Him rightly assumes that we do not have all the answers.

The way up is down. The world will never tell you that. A lot of churches won't even tell you that. In the human realm, it doesn't make sense, but in the heavenly realm, it makes perfect eternal sense. When we go low, God lifts us up.

MEDITATION MOMENT:

If you are physically able, would you bow before the Lord on your knees? Talk to Him about how well you submit to Him, draw near to Him, and humble yourself before Him. Be honest with Him, then ask Him to speak to you about areas of your life that need a bit of work in one of these categories. While you are down there, ask Him to help you be aware of and resist Satan's tricks and lies. What we are doing here is such important heart work. Please do not pass over it.

WEEK FIVE

The Tongue

To say I didn't know it was coming would be a blatant lie. I did. The Holy Spirit had been at work, gently convicting me over the less-than-loving words I used to talk about another person. I thought I could ignore that tap-tap of conviction from the Holy Spirit concerning my flat-out disobedience. I'm not sure whether that was naive or stupid!

Lo, what is that I hear? I believe it was God saying, "Girl, we are going to deal with this whether you like it or not." And deal with it we did!

Over this week of our study, I will share a story of how God made me painfully aware of the destructiveness of the tongue, my tongue. He used several verses from James to drive this point home, and we will look at those this week. Let's go right to them because they are our memory verses for this week.

Please write **James 3:8–10** in the space below. I know I am asking you to memorize three verses this week, but these three verses will be crucial to our time together.

Recipe

Are you a fan of coconut? Perhaps you have a family member who is all about coconut? Most of my family are fans of all things coconut, but none more so than my sweet father-in-law. This week's recipe is one that I consistently make for his birthday, and he loves it. Of course, his birthday might be my excuse for making it so I can eat it also.

I think many cooks never attempt to make a layer cake because it seems complicated to them. The truth is that it is easy to make, and the Coconut Cream Cheese frosting, y'all. Sure, it takes a bit more time than using a boxed cake mix, but I guarantee you will draw rave reviews for this luscious cake.

RECIPE — Leah's Coconut Layer Cake

- 1 cup (2 sticks) **butter**, softened
- 2 cups **sugar**
- 4 **eggs**
- 3 cups all purpose **flour**
- 2 teaspoons **baking powder**
- ½ teaspoon **salt**
- 2 teaspoon **vanilla extract** OR 1 teaspoon **vanilla** and 1 teaspoon **coconut flavoring**
- 1 cup **milk**

Preheat oven to 350°F.

Using parchment paper, cut two pieces that will fit into the bottom of two 9-inch round layer pans.

Cream together butter and sugar until light and fluffy. Add eggs and beat in. Combine flour, baking powder, and salt. Add flour mixture to batter, alternately with milk, and mix until flour is just incorporated. Stir in flavorings.

Divide batter into two 9-inch round, greased and floured, layer pans that have the parchment paper liners in the bottom. Bake 25–30 minutes at 350°F. When done, remove pans from oven and allow to cool for 15 minutes. Turn layers out on a cooling rack, remove the liner from bottom of the cake layer, and cool completely.

RECIPE — Coconut Cream Cheese Frosting

- 11 oz. **cream cheese**
- ⅔ cup **butter**, softened
- 4 ⅓ cups **confectioner's sugar**
- 1 ¼ teaspoon **coconut extract**
- 2 cups **flaked coconut,** toasted

In a bowl, beat cream cheese and butter until fluffy. Add confectioner's sugar and coconut extract. Beat until smooth.

Place one cake layer on a cake plate. Spread ½ cup frosting on the layer, then sprinkle with ⅓ cup coconut. Repeat with the second layer. Spread remaining frosting over top and sides of the cake. Sprinkle with remaining coconut. Refrigerate for 2 hours before cutting. Store in the fridge.

DAY 1

My story continues...

I sat at lunch chatting with two friends from my Tuesday morning Bible study. In the course of the conversation, one of them asked about some less than favorable changes that had taken place in an organization to which I belonged. I had been in the organization long enough and had been close enough to the leader to know that he was the reason for the issues that plagued the organization. I was also very close to several people who had been hurt by the situation. Indeed, my heart had been one of those injured by the leader's actions.

As I answered my friend's question, I laid the blame squarely on the leader, and I did not hold back my feelings. I told my friends some of the things he had done and how numerous people had been hurt and left the organization. While I did not realize until later how deeply hurt and angry I was over the whole mess, my friends told me that my hurt was painfully obvious.

Although our focus verses for today are not ones the Lord used to correct my sinful behavior at the time, He easily could have. Please write **James 1:26–27** in the space below, then use a highlighter or pen to highlight verse 26.

As I prepared to write today's study, my heart was overtaken by conviction from James 1:26. I pondered all the times I have used words carelessly, or with the intent to hurt. My heart broke because of the negative impact those words likely had on my witness for Christ.

James' words are potent here. He says that if I cannot control my tongue, I am deceiving myself to think that my religion or witness is genuine. It is almost more than I can bear to type and admit that my witness may be worthless in the face of unbridled words.

What does that do to you? How does that affect your heart? Take a moment to ponder your desire to represent Christ well and how your words may render that representation worthless. Jot down any thoughts that come to you in the space below.

Today, I would like for us to take time to examine what the Scriptures say about our tongue and the use of our words. I am going to give you Scripture references. Please read each one; then, in the space below the reference, note what it says in your own words. Jot down anything the Holy Spirit speaks into your heart about how the scripture might apply to your own life.

Please do not rush through this exercise. It would be easy to look at this list of scriptures and rush through them to check off that you completed this day of study. Allow the Holy Spirit the time and space to work, my friend.

Psalm 34:13

Psalm 39:1

Psalm 139:4

Proverbs 10:31–32

Proverbs 12:19, 22

Proverbs 15:1–2, 4

Proverbs 17:28

Proverbs 18:7

Proverbs 18:13

Proverbs 18:21

Proverbs 29:20

Isaiah 6:1–7

Matthew 12:34–37

God has strong words to say about how we use our tongues and our words, doesn't He?

MEDITATION MOMENT:

In light of all we have uncovered in the Scriptures concerning our tongue, words, and heart, would you write out a personal prayer that echoes the work of the Spirit in your heart through our time in the Word today?

DAY 2

My story continues...

My friends and I finished lunch, and I got in my car to go home. Suddenly, a dump truck load of conviction from the Holy Spirit hit me head-on. The realization that I had sinned horribly by allowing my hurt and anger to drive my words was overwhelming. It would be nice to say such words had been a one-time occurrence, but they were not. I had spoken in the same angry, hurt tone about the leader to other people on many occasions. My heart was broken over the way I had compromised my testimony and caused others to look down on Jesus—heartbroken at the pain my poisonous words had caused other people!

I texted my two friends, confessed what I had done, and asked for their forgiveness, which they lovingly granted. I thought that would be the end of it. How wrong I was!

The Holy Spirit made it crystal clear that it was time to deal with this sin of negative words. I had no idea how often negative words about all kinds of subjects spewed out of my mouth, but I was about to find out.

God prescribed a three-pronged method for doing away with poison words. Now that I had confessed my sin to God and my friends, I would use prayer, Scripture memory, and oh dear Gussie—accountability, to rein in my tongue.

Confession, both private and public, was the beginning; but, as you will see, confession would be necessary several times over the next 30 days. Each time I allowed poison words to spew forth, I prayed and asked forgiveness. The Lord was faithful to forgive me, encourage my heart to get back in the game, and turn over control of my heart and tongue to the Holy Spirit. Slowly, my need for confession decreased because the spewing of hateful, hurtful, negative words lessened.

For the Scripture memorization, the Lord led me to the Book of James and used a neon highlighter to show me four verses that I was to memorize over the next month. Today, we will focus on three of those verses. Please read **James 3:1–10**, then write **verses 8–10** in the space below.

8 –

9 –

10 –

Now, let's think through this powerful teaching from James. Please answer the following questions:

While **James 3:1–12** is about the tongue, James opens with a sentence that does not seem to fit with the rest of the passage. Why do you think he chooses to toss out a couple of dozen words to teachers?

In this passage, James uses many metaphors from nature and commerce. Please list them here, then circle the one that speaks most clearly to your heart on the topic of the powerful tongue.

How is the tongue described in **verse 6**?

Verse 8 is where the rubber meets the road. How many humans can be successful at taming their tongue?

How is the tongue described in **verse 8**?

Verse 9 outlines two ways the tongue is used. What are they?

Also, in **verse 9**, James uses a phrase to describe people. What is that phrase?

The Greek word used by James for the word likeness is *homoiosis*, and it means resemblance. Only in this verse, however, does it lend the idea of the very image of God being in humans. So, if we bless God and then curse people who contain the image of God, who are we really cursing?

Y'all, I knew those verses. I had read them many times, but the Word suddenly came alive in my heart! The more I repeated James 3:8, the more grieved I became over my negative words. My tongue truly was a restless evil, full of deadly poison. Me! A woman in ministry, for heaven's sake. I had a tongue that

eviscerated other people, and that included my loved ones, on occasion. The horrid part of it was that up till now, I had not felt one bit bad about it. Well, maybe a little bit bad. Suddenly, I understood what the apostle Paul meant when he lamented that he was the chief of sinners. Me, too, Paul. Me, too.

Tomorrow I will share with you the next step in my journey toward a tongue that is more pleasing to God. I hope you will join me.

MEDITATION MOMENT

Since the Bible is clear that no humans can tame their tongue, I feel permitted to ask: How is your tongue? How often do you use it to bless God and curse people? Have you given the Holy Spirit control of your tongue, or has today's lesson been used by the Lord to cause conviction to well up in your heart? I encourage you to talk to Jesus about it and journal whatever you need to in the space below.

DAY 3

My story continues...

Remember my two friends who were the unfortunate recipients of my negative words at lunch that day? Well, the Holy Spirit instructed me to ask them if they would be willing to be my accountability partners in my journey toward sweeter words. Here is the email I sent to my two friends.

> *Good morning,*
>
> *The Holy Spirit troubled my spirit deeply over my actions and words yesterday. I have asked for forgiveness from Him and you, and I know that I have received it. Yet, I feel there is an action He is prompting me to take, and I am coming to you for help.*
>
> *I have a question for you. And please know, upfront, that it is perfectly okay if you need to say no—I promise! I'm looking for some accountability *just* for the month of March in regard to making the words of my mouth acceptable to God (Psalm 19:14).*
>
> *Consistently over the course of my 52 years, my mouth has gotten me in trouble by not speaking the truth IN LOVE, speaking when I should not, saying things that are not kind, etc. Yesterday was evidence that I am in great need of a work of the Holy Spirit in this area. My plan is to be diligent in prayer about this and really seek God's help in controlling my tongue every day. I recognize that my words are a choice, and I must choose not to let my tongue be out of control.*
>
> *I believe that if I can be focused on prayer and effort for the month of March, then controlling my words will become a habit that I can more easily continue. This is where I am asking for your help. Would you be willing to receive a very short email or text from me each morning for the month of March, where I can tell you if I was successful in controlling my tongue the previous day? And if I wasn't, I can tell you why I think I was not. A few sentences, max. I promise not to waste your time in this. Again, if you do not feel led or feel like you can do this, I understand entirely. Thank you for considering it.*

Both of my friends said, "Yes." So beginning on March 2, I reported in every morning with my success, or lack thereof, in my efforts to eliminate poisonous words from my life. It is incredible what accountability will do for an effort like this. I knew that I had to report in, and I hated like everything to have to report failure, so I was much more aware of my words throughout the day. There were a few days when the report was less than stellar, but there were also many wonderfully successful days.

I learned that in life, there are times when negative words must be spoken simply because of circumstances, but they can be expressed without anger and hurt as their fuel. (You must be wondering "Didn't she already know that?) I also became much more aware of my thoughts and where negativity was creeping in BEFORE those thoughts became words.

I am happy to report that speaking grace-filled words, or just keeping my mouth shut completely, happens far more often than speaking negative words these days. I still have moments when I slip and speak a negative word, but the Holy Spirit convicts me immediately, and I confess my sin. I will likely be a work in progress until the day God takes me home to heaven, but I'm so thankful He took me down this path.

So, why all the words about accountability? Glad you asked. Let's begin with reading **Jeremiah 17:9**. What does the Lord, through the prophet Jeremiah, tell us about the heart?

What does it mean that the heart is deceitful?

The bottom line is that our hearts cannot be trusted to tell us the truth. My heart had convinced my head that the hurt and anger I felt was sufficient justification for spewing negative words about the leader. Thus, I felt no guilt over those words, and I justified them because they were true.

See how sneaky that is? Even though I never told an untruth about this man and his actions, I had no business trying to make him look bad in the eyes of others. My words were sinful.

Let's finish up in **Ecclesiastes 4** and see what Solomon has to say about accountability. Please read **verses 9–12**.

What are the three things Solomon says about being alone and without accountability and help?

There are four things Solomon says about having a friend to walk with you through life. What are they?

I am convinced to the core of my soul that my healing from negative words would not have been as profound without the accountability I received from God and my friends. Sure, there are times when I mess up, and words slip from my mouth that are negative or hurtful, but each time the Spirit reminds me of the work I did and helps me sweeten my words. Accountability brings awareness, and awareness facilitates awakening of the spirit to a new way of walking and talking.

MEDITATION MOMENT:

Who or what do you trust more when it comes to your words and actions—your heart or God's Holy Spirit?

Are you guilty, like I was, of justifying sinful behavior?

Do you have an accountability partner?

Is there an area of your life where you might benefit from an accountability partner with whom you can be completely transparent?

DAY 4

My story continues...

The more diligent I was about replacing my negative words about other people with the truth of Scripture, the more sensitive I became to the whispers of the Holy Spirit.

One day in the middle of my month of accountability, I decided to read through the Book of James. When my reading brought me to chapter 5, the Spirit tossed up a STOP sign at verse 9 and said, "We have more work to do."

Before I finish my story, please turn to **James 4:11–12** and **James 5:9**. Write these verses in the space below.

While James 5:9 is the verse the Lord used to refine me further, I want us to pair it with the first sentence of James 4:11. Please highlight or underline these passages.

When I read James 5:9, my heart was immediately convicted of the grumbling that had become such a part of my life that I didn't even realize I was doing it, or at least did not know that it was so detrimental to my faith.

The conviction I felt was not concerning my negative words about the leader. God and I had already dealt with that. The grumbling about which I felt conviction was directed toward my precious husband and other loved ones, and it was usually a criticism that took place inside my head.

Am I stepping on anyone's toes yet?

The Greek word used for grumble carries the idea of murmuring or groaning inwardly, precisely what I had been doing when someone was not acting the way I thought he or she should act. Suddenly, I understood how much of a faith-buster murmuring is. I discovered that when I murmur against another person, it usually means that I feel superior to them and look down on them in some way. That, my friend, screams of pride, and God is clear in the Scriptures that He hates pride.

Murmuring and grumbling end up consuming our thoughts, leaving no room for the truth of God. One grumble turns into another and another, and soon, the perceived offense against me consumes my thoughts. In that situation, it is very easy for grumbling to become a stronghold.

Let's go back now to James 4:11. The ESV translation of the Bible says that we should *not speak evil against one another, brothers*. James is addressing believers who have been speaking evil or slandering other believers.

How are the words *grumble* and *speak evil* related, you might ask? I believe with all my heart that if I give into grumbling or groaning in my thoughts against a fellow believer, it is an easy transition into verbal slandering and maligning of that person. Neither grumbling or slandering bless God.

Let's do a bit of investigative work to see other places in Scripture where the following words, or variations of them, are used:

- Grumble
- Complain
- Slander

Look up the following verses and note what they say about these words:

Psalm 50:19–21

Psalm 101:5

Proverbs 10:18

1 Corinthians 10:1–11

Galatians 5:14–15 (Note: Some very vivid words are used in these verses to depict slander.)

Philippians 2:14

Jude 3—4 and 16

Let's finish with **Psalm 139:4**. Please turn there, read the verse, then write it in the space below.

I don't know about you, but that verse slays me. All my bad-mouthin', my grumbling, complaining, and yes, even slandering other people, God knew about it all before it was ever poured forth from my lips. He knew what I would say, why I would say it, and what effects it would have on other people and me.

Y'all, our words have power! Power to lift or destroy. Power to encourage or discourage. Power to grow faith or tear it down. Words are powerful, and I want to use mine well. How about you?

MEDITATION MOMENT:

Today I want to do something a bit different in our meditation time. I love fresh starts and new beginnings, and I want us to experience those concerning our words. On a separate piece of paper, begin making a list of every time you can recall using your words in ways that were not pleasing to God. Don't rush through this. Ask the Lord to bring to mind any hurtful words you have spoken... hurtful to other people or harmful to yourself. (You do know that we say disparaging things to ourselves that we would never say to others, don't you?)

Here are some possible examples to get you started.

- Lying
- Talking about others behind their back
- Failing to keep something confidential after being asked to do so
- Angry words about someone, or to someone, who hurt you
- Gossip

Once you have your list, spend some time with Jesus over it. Confess your sin and ask Him to forgive you if you have not previously requested forgiveness. Ask the Holy Spirit to help you do whatever is necessary to repent and go in a new direction with your words. If God requires you to speak an apology to another person, do it quickly before Satan talks you out of it.

Because God removes our confessed and covered sins as far as the east is from the west, I want you to destroy your list in some way. Burn it, shred it, flush it, put it in a balloon and send it away into the heavens. Whatever method signifies a completed work of forgiveness and a fresh start to you, do it.

Finally, I would love to hear from you. Please email me at info@leahadams.org and share how the Lord worked in your heart through this particular Meditation Moment.

DAY 5

Many years ago, a man asked me how I knew if a mutual acquaintance was lying. When I did not answer immediately, he said, "You know he is lying when his lips are moving." Regardless of whether what he said was true, I found it to be such a sad statement about the person's character.

Please turn to **James 5:12** and write it in the space below.

My daddy earned a living as a real estate developer in our small north Georgia community. A drive through the county reveals numerous buildings and developments on which his fingerprint remains. Now that he is with Jesus, my sister and I own the buildings and engage with our renters.

My daddy was a man of his word. His "yes" meant yes, and his "no" meant no. With only one exception, Daddy never required those renting commercial space from him to sign a lease. All of his dealings were done based on his word and a handshake. Even today, the situation remains the same. All of our tenants have rented from our family for over 15 years, and some closer to 25 years. We do not have formal written leases with any of our tenants.

In ancient Israel, an oath that was sworn by a Jewish person usually involved invoking the name of God. So, given the fact that devout Jews did not even speak the name "God," it was a huge deal to swear by His name. The person swearing the oath had better be committed to fulfilling that oath at the risk of his very life.

Let's take a look at a few passages that James might have been pondering when he wrote verse 12. Please read each passage and answer the accompanying questions.

In **Leviticus 19:12**, God tells His people what they have done when they swear an oath using His name and then do not keep it. How is this described and what is the result?

To swear falsely would be to make God's name common, and yes, unholy. How many times, in casual conversation, have you heard someone say, "I swear to God!" You know immediately that there is nothing holy about the manner in which they are using God's name. Taking an oath in God's name no longer holds the esteem and seriousness that it should.

Of what are we guilty if we swear an oath (make a vow) to God and do not fulfill it, according to **Deuteronomy 23:21**?

We have made common the holy name of God when we make a vow or an oath in His name and do not keep that oath or vow. We are guilty of sin.

Now, let's listen to the words of our Lord on this topic. Please turn to **Matthew 5** and read **verses 33–37**.

What instruction does Jesus give His followers in **verse 34**, and again in **verse 36**, that is different than the warning given by God in the Old Testament?

Do NOT take an oath at all. Jesus leaves no room for equivocation. Just don't do it. He knew that you and I are woefully unequipped to keep all our oaths and vows. We are! When over 50% of marriages end in divorce, our promise-keeping track record stinks.

What does He say we should say in the place of oaths?

Yes or No. That's it.

Now, let's turn to **Titus 2** and consider how we can be simple yes or no people whose character is above reproach and whose word is trusted to be true.

In Titus 2:1–8, we find Paul instructing Titus on the best way to grow up a godly community that is above reproach. Please read the specific verses referenced and fill in the answers to the question associated with those verses.

Paul takes a top-down approach and begins with Titus. List every instruction that Paul gives **Titus in verses 1, 7, and 8**, concerning how he is to live his life and serve in ministry.

What traits are older men to exhibit, according to **verse 2**?

Interestingly, older women are charged with exhibiting godly character AND training younger women. What traits are the older women to display according to **verse 3**?

List the training the older women should give to the younger women.

Before we move on, I feel the hair going up on some necks over Paul's choice of wording regarding "working at home." I do not believe Paul was forbidding working outside the home. There are examples in the Bible of women who worked outside the home; i.e., Ruth gleaned the fields, Priscilla was a tentmaker.

Take a look at **1 Timothy 5:14**, where it says that women are to manage their home. The Greek word used here is one that implies that the woman is the heart of the home, the hub in the middle of the "home wheel."

We have power, girls. Because God made us the heart of the home, we have the power to set the tone in our homes. That can be work sometimes, but it is work to which God has called us.

Finally, what kind of training is **Titus** to give the younger men in **verses 6 and 7**?

Now, go back and look at your lists. If Christ-followers were to teach sound doctrine, be sober/serious-minded, self-controlled, faithful, reverent in our behavior, not slandering other people, not bound by alcohol or drugs, pure, kind, submissive, walking in integrity, with dignity and sound speech, what kind of witness would we have for the cause of Christ? The world would know that we are trustworthy, honest, and true; that our "yes" is yes, and our "no" is no.

I don't know about you, but I want to be a woman who does not need to swear an oath to make people trust her and believe her. I want to live the kind of life that testifies to the world that I am trustworthy and dependable.

Do you want to know why I desire that so much? Return to **Titus 2:4–5** and read these verses. What should be our motivation for living a life that is pleasing to God?

I don't know about you, but I would rather die than disgrace the Word of God and my Lord by my actions and words. Oh, I've done it plenty of times, and plenty of times, God has forgiven me for it. Yet, my heart desires cleanness and purity before God, so no one has a reason to look down on the Word because of my actions.

You and I have everything we need for life and godliness (2 Peter 1:3). Let's allow today's lesson to take up residence in our hearts and move us to be people whose "yes" is yes and whose "no" is no.

MEDITATION MOMENT:

Do you know men and women who would fit the description of "yes" is yes, and "no" is no people? What can you learn from them? Study their lives, talk to them, if possible. Allow their lives to mentor you so that you can, one day, mentor a younger person by the way you live your life.

WEEK SIX

Dear God, I Want It Now!

Hi there! Can you believe this is our final week of study with James, our mentor? What a journey this has been! James has indeed been a friend to us because he has been willing not only to encourage us on our faith walk, but also to correct us in places where we have strayed off the path. He has been willing to say the hard things to us, and we all need that kind of person in our life.

This week, James ends his letter by reminding us of the importance and power of prayer. I can think of no better way for us to conclude our study than with a focus on prayer. But, before James speaks about prayer, he reminds us of the importance of patience.

Agh, the "P" word. Why didn't James stick with prayer instead of getting all up in my kitchen with the topic of patience? Stink! Could it be because most people, Christians included, need to do some work in the area of patience? Remember, James started his letter addressing the need for patience, or steadfastness, and now he ends his message with the same.

I do not know about you, but I want to take in all that the Holy Spirit is seeking to teach me, so let's walk into this week of lessons with an open heart. Teach us, Lord.

Our memory verse for this week is **James 5:16b**. Please write it in the space below.

Recipe

What dessert comes to mind when you think about summer celebrations? For me, it is homemade ice cream. I have lovely memories from my childhood of my parents making homemade ice cream in the summer. Very often, friends and family would gather at our home and enjoy vanilla or strawberry ice cream that my mother had made in our very noisy electric ice cream freezer. It was so good.

Several years ago, I was deep into a conversation with a fellow pharmacist at work about trying to find a delicious homemade ice cream recipe. So many recipes yield an icy ice cream, rather than a smooth and creamy one. Roy looked at me and said, "I have the best recipe for homemade vanilla ice cream. I promise you won't find a better one."

Well, that is all I needed to prompt me to say, "Please share the recipe." He did, and he was right. It truly is the very best homemade ice cream I have ever eaten. I hope you will agree.

RECIPE

Roy's Homemade Vanilla Ice Cream

2 cups **whole milk**

1¾ cups **white sugar**

½ teaspoon **salt**

2 cups **half and half**

1 tablespoon **pure vanilla extract**

4 cups **whipping cream**

Scald the whole milk in a pan until bubbles form. Remove pan from heat and add in remaining ingredients. Stir until combined, cover the pan, and refrigerate for 30 minutes.

Place mixture into freezer portion of ice cream maker and make according to your ice cream maker's directions.

NOTE: you can add in any fruit or other ingredients you would like after the mixture has chilled.

DAY 1

In preparation for writing today's lesson, I did a brief survey on my Facebook page to determine if what I assumed to be true about patience was, in fact, true.

The poll asked my friends this question: "Do you consider yourself to be a patient person?"

The respondents had two answers from which to choose:

"Yes, being patient comes easy for me."
"No, I definitely need to work on patience."

In an almost 3 to 1 margin, those admitting that they need to work on patience outpaced those who seemingly have mastered it. I was not surprised that the majority of people agreed that patience does not come easily for them. I would have to say that I fall somewhere in the middle. In many, many instances, I am quite patient; yet, there are plenty of times when a dose of patience would benefit me. So, I think today's lesson will be a good one for all of us.

The verses on which we will focus today are found in **James 5**. Specifically, we will camp in **verses 7–8**. Would you write them in the space below?

James begins by saying, *Be patient, therefore, brothers*. Anytime the word "therefore" is used, it is important to ask one question: "What is it 'there for'?"

James is using *therefore* to connect what he is about to say to what he just said. So, when we refer back to the verses just before verse 7, we discover that James has reprimanded the rich people who oppress others. In light of his warnings to those who are wealthy, James now seeks to encourage the believers to have patience amid persecution.

In verses 7–8, James takes the long view of the circumstances under which his Christian brothers and sisters are living when he tells them to be patient until the coming of the Lord.

Why do you think James tells his readers this?

Virtually all Christians, at some time in their lives, will face some level of persecution and trial. It may be as mild as someone making fun of us for believing in Jesus, or it might involve the risk of death because of our faith in Christ. We must keep a proper perspective when persecution and trials come along.

Go with me, please, to a few scriptures, and let's see what we can learn about the time of Christ's return to which James makes reference and how looking ahead to that day can help us have patience. Please read the referenced passage and answer the question that accompanies it.

When other people persecute us for our faith, who or what is the source of the persecution, according to **Ephesians 6:12**?

What words of comfort can we rest on from **Psalm 103:6**?

In the Book of Revelation, Jesus speaks words to the seven churches through John. To each of the churches, Christ sends a message, either of condemnation or confirmation. Included in most of the messages to the churches are specific words of encouragement to those who hold fast to the faith and overcome the persecution of the day. What will the overcomers receive according to the following passages?

Revelation 2:7

Revelation 2:10

Revelation 2:17

Revelation 2:26–28

Revelation 3:5

Revelation 3:10 and 12

Revelation 3:21

That is quite a list of rewards, wouldn't you say? Continuing our look at the coming of the Lord, please turn to **Revelation 19:11–16** and write out a description of Christ and what He will accomplish when He returns.

Death, hell, and the grave will be silenced once and for all when Christ returns to the earth. Jesus will make all things new and right, according to **Revelation 21:1–8**. Please read this passage slowly and carefully. Make a list of the evidence from these verses that wrong will be righted and every moment of persecution will become a distant memory.

Be patient, friends, until the coming of the Lord. Jesus modeled this for us when He suffered and died on the cross. The writer of Hebrews 12 reminds us that *for the joy that was set before him Jesus endured the cross* (Hebrews 12:2). He knew the cross was temporary, but His throne in heaven would be eternal. The pain and ridicule and the weight of sin heaped upon Him were temporary, but unbroken fellowship with God and with those who would accept Him as Lord and Savior would be eternal.

This is our mandate, sweet friend. When times are tough and there is more tunnel than light; when there seems to be no justice for the wrongs committed in this world; when persecution comes knocking on your door, be patient, endure, and keep your eyes on Jesus for the joy set before you.

> *He will wipe away every tear from their eyes, and death shall be no more, neither shall there be mourning, nor crying, nor pain anymore, for the former things have passed away.* Revelation 21:4

Given this, be patient, dear sisters, until Jesus returns.

MEDITATION MOMENT:

Are you in the middle of a trial right now? Are you experiencing persecution because you are a believer in Jesus Christ? If you answered "yes" to either of these questions, what actions might you take to encourage your patience and establish your heart? What reminders from the Scriptures might you use to preach encouragement to your heart when nothing seems to be going right?

DAY 2

Life is difficult, people are difficult, and sometimes God is silent until He is not.

Now, aren't you excited about Bible study today?

As our study of the Book of James draws to a close, we once again find James talking about patience in suffering. Nowhere in the Bible do we have a worthier example of that than in the Book of Job. Our opening statement for today pretty much sums up the life of Job. Oh, not the beginning of his life, nor the end, but the middle years. The man endured unspeakable loss, yet maintained his faith in his God through it all.

Let's begin our day by writing out **James 5:10–11** in the space below.

The first thought that blasts its way out of my mind when I read verse 11 is, "Are you kidding me? The words blessed, compassionate, and merciful do not seem to fit at all in the story of Job." But, the Scriptures say they do, so I will trust God's wisdom.

Two words are used in the Bible for *patience*. The first is *hypomone*, used in verse 11, and it means to bear up under trial that comes because of circumstances. The second word used in Scripture for *patience*, or *perseverance*, is *makrothymia* which carries the idea of patience with people.

Job needed a heaping helping of both kinds of patience, as we will see today. There are three concepts that I want us to explore from Job's life, all of which I summed up in my opening statement.

Life Is Difficult

Please read **Job 1:2—2:10**. Sketch out a basic profile of Job and the circumstances of this passage using the outline in the space below.

Job, the man

Events in heaven

Tragedies that happened to Job

The Bible describes our friend, Job, as blameless and upright. I know what you are thinking, but blameless does not mean perfect. So let's get that out of the way first.

I heard a pastor explain the word blameless in this way: "Nothing to hide, nothing to fear." Job had nothing to hide concerning his life, marriage, family, and business. Therefore, Job had nothing to fear. All too often, fear is born out of secrets and deception. None of that was going on in Job's life, which makes what happened to Job even more challenging to understand.

You see, you and I have the benefit of knowing in advance what Job likely never knew...that God was so confident in Job's faith He allowed Job to go through horrible tragedy to prove the genuineness of that faith. You and I can see that there is glory in Job's story because we know the end of the story. Job did not have that benefit in the heat of the crucible. Neither do we when we are walking through the fire. We simply must trust that God does all things well.

People Are Difficult

Each of us has those difficult people in our lives, the ones I like to call "sandpaper people." Every time they breathe, they irritate us. Their words and behavior prove to be a source of aggravation.

Don't look at me all "holier than thou"! You have those kind of people in your life, and I do too. So did Job. Let's read on.

Read Job 2:11–13 and write the names of Job's friends in the space below.

According to these verses, what was their stated purpose in coming to visit Job?

It all started pretty well. They came, they mourned, they kept him company, and no one said a word. If only they had continued in their silence, but their tongues soon spewed evidence of what was in their hearts.

Let's begin with Eliphaz, the Temanite. What words of comfort did he offer Job in his suffering in **Job 4:7–9 and 17**? How would you describe Eliphaz's attitude toward Job?

After Job replies to Eliphaz, Bildad, the Shuhite, steps to the microphone next. Read **Job 8:1–7** and describe his words of comfort and his attitude toward Job.

With friends like these, who needs enemies, right? As if poor Job had not already suffered enough, here comes Zophar, the Naamathite. Read **Job 11:1–6** and, once again, write out an overview of Zophar's words to Job and his attitude toward Job.

Multiple rounds of this torture continue as each so-called friend speaks and Job replies, maintaining his innocence before God. These men are legalistic, judgmental, and condemning. None of them have walked in Job's sandals, nor have they sat in his ash heap.

We must be very careful to comfort and not condemn those who are suffering and enduring trial and tragedy. We have not sat in their ash heap, and we have no business judging or condemning them.

Most of the time, the only thing a suffering person truly needs from another human is presence. They need us to be God-with-skin-on, bringing peace and comfort and a shoulder on which they can cry. The reality is that very rarely can we right the wrong that afflicts those who suffer. We simply need to sit with them, cry with them, listen to them, and pray with and for them.

God Is Silent Until He Is Not

Anyone familiar with the Book of Job knows that it is 38 chapters into Job's suffering before God breaks His silence, and when He does He holds nothing back.

How does God begin His portion of the conversation with Job in **Job 38:2**?

Say what? Is God really talking to Job, or is He addressing Job's friends?

I want us to do a quick overview of God's address to Job. Please look up the following scriptures and note the questions God poses to Job.

Job 38:4

Job 38:12–13

Job 38:32

Job 39:19–20

Job 40:1–2

Job 40:6–8

Why in the world would God address Job as if Job were as sinful as his friends had accused him of being? God's attitude is downright condescending! Ah, but God has a plan and a purpose.

In Charles Swindoll's excellent book entitled *Job: A Man of Heroic Endurance*, he states:

> It seems that the Lord is helping Job get beyond his immediate world of hurt—his ever-present counselors with their never-ending criticism and blame. By doing this, He is preparing Job's heart, if you will, for a new understanding of His ways, for a willingness to forgive those men of their harsh words, and for the ability to recover and go on without bitterness or other inner scars. [13]

God's words to Job might have hurt him, but they did not harm him. In the end, God's rebuke of Job accomplished what God intended.

What was Job's response in **Job 40:3–5**?

Take a look at Job's final words to God in **Job 42:1–6**. Even though God proclaimed Job blameless and righteous, God knew there was still work to do in Job's heart.

Job came out of his season of tragedy and trial, not with a heart full of bitterness, but with a heart more fully submitted to God and His sovereignty.

We can learn much from Job that applies to the trials and tragedies that you and I endure. To learn and grow from our difficult times, we must be willing to allow God to work in the ways He knows will best accomplish His purposes. This is what faith is all about.

MEDITATION MOMENT:

Job's story does not end with his repentance before God. In **Job 42:10–17**, we see that Job's life has come full circle. Take a moment to read this passage and note how God restored all that Job had lost. What does this tell you about God? About Job? How might you apply this full-circle truth to your own life?

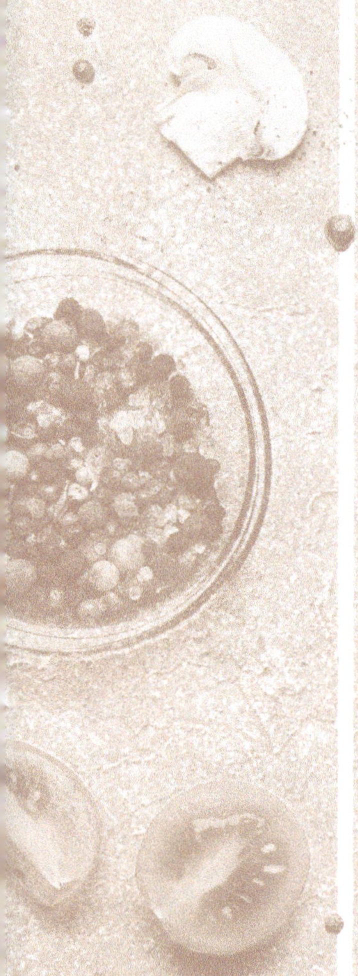

DAY 3

If you grew up in the church, as I did, you are likely familiar with the midweek service known as the prayer meeting. For our tiny congregation, prayer meeting was held on Wednesday night and consisted of a song, a few minutes of prayer over a prayer list that was handed out, and finally a short message by the pastor. The midweek service was such a staple in the life of our church that I was into my thirties before I ever questioned the fact that the time spent in actual prayer during the meeting was a relatively small portion of the hour.

In 1972 in the heart of Brooklyn, New York, Jim Cymbala and his wife Carol were struggling to pastor a church that was on the brink of closing its doors. The building was dilapidated, the pews were literally breaking in two while people sat on them, and the bank account was in the red more often than not.

In his book, *Fresh Wind, Fresh Fire,* Cymbala tells the story of contemplating the newest church growth strategies of the day in a desperate attempt to save the dying congregation from extinction. Most of the ideas required an investment of finances; however, the church budget was already on life support, so options were very limited.

At his lowest point, Cymbala was visiting his in-laws in Florida and was invited to go on a deep-sea fishing trip. His desperation over his congregation was so great that he cried out to God for help, even as he fished. He writes:

> "Lord, I have no idea how to be a successful pastor," I prayed softly out there on the water. "I haven't been trained. All I know is that Carol and I are working in the middle of New York City, with people dying on every side, overdosing from heroin, consumed by materialism, and all the rest. If the gospel is so powerful..."
>
> I couldn't finish the sentence. Tears choked me. Fortunately, the others on the boat were too far away to notice as they studied their lines in the blue-green water.
>
> Then quietly but forcefully, in words heard not with my ear but deep within my spirit, I sensed God speaking:
>
> "If you and your wife will lead my people to pray and call upon my name, you will never lack for something fresh to preach. I will supply all the

money that's needed, both for the church and for your family, and you will never have a building large enough to contain the crowds I will send in response."[14]

Jim went back to New York and told his tiny congregation that from that day forward the Tuesday night prayer service, rather than the Sunday morning worship service, would be the cornerstone of Brooklyn Tabernacle's ministry.

If you know anything about the Brooklyn Tabernacle church, you know that God kept His promise to Cymbala. Within weeks, the church began to grow and come alive because of what happened on Tuesday nights. Cymbala says, "We were not there to hear one another give voice to eloquent prayers; we were too desperate for that. We focused vertically, on God, rather than horizontally on one another."[15]

I am convinced that the American church has not yet begun to understand and use the power available to us from God through prayer. In our time together today, James will call us into a deeper prayer life so that we can be more effective in God's kingdom. Please turn to **James 5:13–15**. Read these verses carefully, then write them in the space below.

It is critical that we take a couple of minutes and remind ourselves of the context of these verses. For the preceding 12 verses, James has encouraged his readers to remain faithful to Christ in good times as well as when they endure persecution. So, the topic of suffering in verse 13 is a natural progression from the preceding verses.

Verse 13 describes two groups of people who are being encouraged to pray. How are these two groups described?

[14] Cymbala, Jim, *Fresh Wind, Fresh Fire: What Happens When God's Spirit Invades the Hearts of His People* (Grand Rapids: Zondervan, 1997), 25.

[15] Ibid, 29.

The Greek word used for suffering in verse 13 lends the idea of suffering hardship or trouble, rather than physical suffering. James seems to know individuals in his sphere of influence who are suffering persecution. He tells them to pray.

The cheerful in **verse 13** are told to do what?

Many songs sung in the day in which James wrote this text would have been taken verbatim from the Book of Psalms. Throughout my life, I have learned that there is great power in praying God's Word back to Him, which is what would have been happening as those who were cheerful in the midst of suffering sang songs of praise to God.

Who is James addressing in **verses 14 and 15**?

What instructions does he give to the sick?

Why might James encourage the sick to call for the elders in the church to pray for them? Let's look at **Titus 1:5–9** to give us insight. What characteristics and qualifications did Paul establish for elders and overseers? Focus specifically on **verse 9** and note below what the elders must do.

The elders of a church should be spiritually mature, sound in doctrine and God's Word, and able to seek the will of God for their lives and the lives of their church members.

What I do not believe James is saying in this verse is that everyone who calls the elders of the church to pray over them and anoint them with oil will be healed here on this earth. Nothing in the Bible supports that stance, although it is a popular theology with some.

Let's remind ourselves of the three groups of people James is addressing:

The suffering
The cheerful
The sick

That pretty much covers it, people. Each of us likely falls into one of the three groups at some time in our life. I believe that James is trying to convey that prayer is ALWAYS the right thing to do.

There is power in prayer because there is power in God. Our prayers do not hold the ultimate power, but the One to whom we are praying does.

What does Paul tell us to do in **Philippians 4:6–7**? What guidelines does he give regarding the issues about which we are to pray?

We are to pray about everything, and we are to do it with an attitude of thanksgiving. Friends, if we are commanded to pray about everything, then everything can be affected by prayer. Let's be obedient and become prayer-wielding ninja warriors for Christ. Are you ready?

MEDITATION MOMENT:

Consider how prominent the topic of prayer is in the beautiful old hymn, *What a Friend We Have in Jesus*. If you know this hymn, sing it out loud as an encouragement to your heart, or perhaps find it online and listen to the words as it is sung. I think you will be blessed.

What a Friend we have in Jesus,
  All our sins and griefs to bear!
What a privilege to carry
  Everything to God in prayer!
O what peace we often forfeit,
  O what needless pain we bear,
All because we do not carry
  Everything to God in prayer!

Have we trials and temptations?
  Is there trouble anywhere?
We should never be discouraged,
  Take it to the Lord in prayer.
Can we find a friend so faithful
  Who will all our sorrows share?
Jesus knows our every weakness,
  Take it to the Lord in prayer.

Are we weak and heavy-laden,
  Cumbered with a load of care?
Precious Savior, still our refuge—
  Take it to the Lord in prayer;
Do thy friends despise, forsake thee?
  Take it to the Lord in prayer;
In His arms He'll take and shield thee,
  Thou wilt find a solace there.[16]

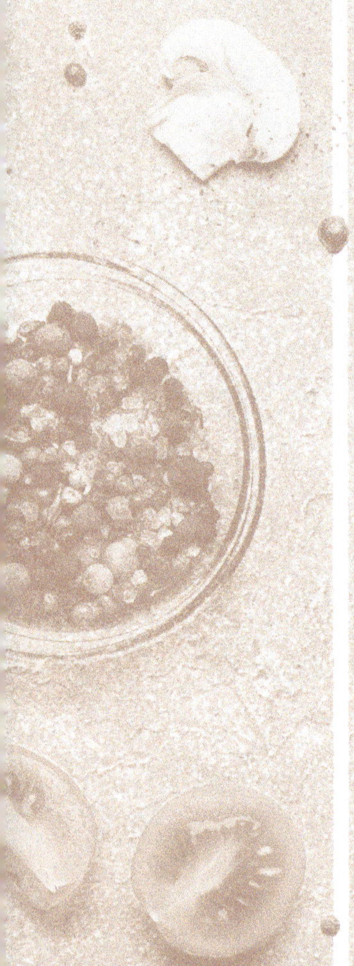

DAY 4

How is your prayer life?

More specifically, are the prayers you offer to the Lord powerful, or are they generic, weak, and ineffective?

For so many years, I was guilty of the latter. I prayed prayers like "Bless them, Lord" or "Help so-and-so, Father." Please do not misunderstand me. I believe that there is a time, place, and circumstance in which generic prayer is acceptable and appropriate. Sometimes we do not know how to pray, and all we can pray is for the Lord to help another person or us. But, sometimes we grow lazy in our praying.

In our time together today, we will find encouragement from James to live in such a way that causes our prayers to be powerful and effective. Please turn to **James 5** and read **verses 16–18** and write them in the space below.

James 5:16 begins with an encouragement to the Christ-followers of James' day, and of ours, to not allow sin against another believer to fester and plant a root of bitterness in the heart. If I have sinned against a brother or sister in Christ, as soon as the Holy Spirit makes me aware of the sin and my need to make things right, I need to go to that person, confess my sin, and ask their forgiveness. Regardless of their response, I will have been obedient to do what God expects of me.

Jesus was very clear about the importance of unity in the body of Christ and how others will be drawn to the faith by that unity. Therefore, we must be quick to say, "I was wrong. Please forgive me." Asking forgiveness for a sin against another believer opens the door to healing of the relationship between you and that person.

Allow me to take a moment and say that I do not believe James is setting a standard of confession to a pastor or priest to obtain forgiveness from God. What standard does **Hebrews 10:19–22** establish for the believer concerning the confession of sin?

Because of what Jesus' death accomplished on the cross, the veil that separated Holy God and sinful men and women in the temple was ripped from top to bottom. You and I now have access to walk freely into God's presence, confess our sin, and receive forgiveness.

So with that said, I want us to consider the final sentence of **verse 16**. Please write it in the space below.

What makes a person righteous? What does the word "righteous" even mean? If you and I are considered to be righteous, that means that we are in right standing before God.

How do we attain right standing before God? We find the answer to that question in **2 Corinthians 5:18–21** and **Romans 5:19**. Note what you see below.

If you have accepted Jesus as your Lord and Savior, then you are declared righteous before God. You may not always feel righteous or act righteously, but the blood of Jesus covers your sins, and you are in right standing with God.

In addition to urging us to pray powerful prayers, James offers us an example of a man who did just that. The prophet Elijah knew a thing or two about prayer. Let's take a little trip around the Scriptures and see if we can discern why Elijah's prayers were so powerful.

Let's begin with what James stated about Elijah in **James 5:17–18**. If you were building a character profile (not a list of accomplishments) of Elijah, what critical information would you pull from these verses?

Please go to **1 Kings 17:1–5** and make notes of any additional points you might add to Elijah's character profile from this passage.

FOR FURTHER STUDY:

Read **1 Kings 17–19** to get a complete picture of the work and life of Elijah.

Elijah is best known for the episode on Mount Carmel with the prophets of Baal, and the resurrection from the dead of the widow's son. Both of these miracles took place because of Elijah's powerful prayers to the miracle-working God He served. I believe there are two characteristics that Elijah possessed that caused God to use him as the conduit through which He performed mighty miracles.

The first one we find in 1 Kings 17:1 when Elijah tells Ahab a drought is coming. Now, anyone could declare a drought to the king, but four words in this sentence set Elijah apart:

Before whom I stand.

Elijah was not a rogue prophet—he took his orders straight from God. Yet, remember that Elijah was no different than you and me. This prophet was a mere mortal, but also a human who knew that he could not stand before kings until he had stood before God. Elijah knew that in his own power, he had no power.

Do you want to pray powerful prayers? Stand before God. Spend time in His Word and listen to His voice. This brings us to the second reason I believe Elijah could pray powerful and effective prayers. Please turn to **1 Kings 18:36–37**. Make a list of the things that Elijah requested from God.

Each time I read this passage, I am struck by the humility of Elijah, and by his desire for God's renown rather than his own. We need more of that in our day—more humility, more desire for God's name to be made known, and a willingness to stand before God before we stand before people. I believe these are the things that set Elijah apart and empowered his prayers. He bowed, he listened, and he prayed.

What is the task to which God has called you? Are you standing before kings? Are you raising little ones? Repairing cars? Helping to heal bodies as a nurse or doctor? Are you working as a correctional officer? Teacher? Police officer? Pastor? Missionary? Farmer? Writer?

Regardless of the task, the question on the table is: "Are you standing before God, listening for His voice, and desiring His renown more than your own?"

Are your prayers powerful and effective because of your intentional, humble positioning of yourself before God?

What would have to change for you to be an Elijah in your generation?

MEDITATION MOMENT:

Would you make **Isaiah 26:8** your prayer today?

DAY 5

Do you want to know what I love most about James, the author? He keeps the main thing the main thing. There are no rabbit trails to chase, no extended greetings or endings, nor any apologies for the hard stuff God charges him with saying to his readers.

James knows that time is short, and people are dying without Christ every single day. Therefore, he wants to say what he needs to say without any frills or confusion. Nowhere is this more apparent than at the end of his letter.

In his final words, James reminds readers of the most important thing they can do as followers of Jesus Christ. Please write **James 5:19–20** in the space below.

These two verses of Scripture have caused no small amount of indigestion among biblical scholars. To whom is James referring when he references someone wandering from the truth? And, is it even necessary that we know the answer to that question?

Recall that the entirety of the Book of James offers commands and encouragement to live the Christian life. I think it is appropriate that James would end his book with a reminder to the believers that their job on this earth is to point people to Jesus. Look closely at **verse 19**! To whom is James addressing these two verses (19–20)?

What we see in this verse is salvation wording, friends. No matter why a person wanders, it is the job of Christians to point them to Jesus. Please turn to Matthew 28:18–20 and note the four commands Jesus gave His followers before He left this earth.

Every person who follows Christ is to:

1. Go
2. Make disciples
3. Baptize them in the name of the Father, the Son, and the Holy Spirit
4. Teach them

Our mandate is to teach those who are new to the Christian faith about Jesus and how to live a life that is pleasing to Him. When the Scriptures are preached and taught, people will be convicted of sin and drawn to Christ. This is how the Church grows and thrives and flourishes.

Now, let's look at two other passages that fit quite nicely with James 5:19–20. Please turn to **2 Corinthians 5:17–19** and answer the following questions:

Because we have been saved, we now have a ministry. How does **verse 18** describe this ministry?

The Apostle Paul clearly described how we are to carry out this ministry of reconciliation in **1 Corinthians 1:17**. What is the tool we are to use to be ministers of reconciliation?

The gospel is the tool of reconciliation. What word did James use in **James 5:19** to describe the gospel?

What or who is the truth, according to **John 14:6?**

It all circles back around to Jesus. James opened his letter with a reference to

Jesus, and he closes with a reference to Jesus. Why?

After years of growing up in the shadow of his big Brother and watching His life; after rejecting Jesus, then returning to Him; after seeing Jesus die on the cross and rise from the grave...after all this, James knew that living the Christian life was the only place where he found real life. It is the same for you and me.

May I be so bold as to say that if you and I have spent six weeks studying the Book of James and we walk away without a renewed commitment to sharing the gospel with those who do not know Jesus or those who have wandered away, we have wasted our time. If our time in James has not encouraged us to live lives that look like Jesus, we might as well have just picked up a good fiction novel and read it.

The Bible is alive and active and has the power to change us and equip us to be ministers of reconciliation in a world that is desperately in need of a Savior. My prayer is that your heart desires to live in such a way, to speak in such a way, to serve in such a way that other people are irresistibly drawn to Christ.

Has your time in the Book of James been life changing? I hope so for it is a magnificent book. Thank you for taking this journey with me. It has been my honor and pleasure to be your Holy Spirit-led teacher.

MEDITATION MOMENT:

What "Ah-ha!" moments have you experienced during your study of James? How has God used the Book of James to strengthen and encourage your faith and your walk? What are your take-away ideas and concepts from this study?

Bibliography

"ABOUT." Rescuing Hope, September 16, 2019. https://www.rescuinghope.com/aboutus/.

Bonhoeffer, Deitrich, *Temptation* (New York: Macmillan Publishing Co., 1953), 116.

Cedar, Paul A., *The Communicator's Commentary: James, 1, 2 Peter, Jude*, ed. By Lloyd J. Ogilvie (Waco, TX: Word Books, 1984),88-89.

Clark, Roy, Gordie Tapp, Grandpa Jones, Archie Campbell, "Gloom, Despair, and Agony," *Hee Haw*, written by Bernie Brillstein, Frank Peppiatt, and John Aylesworth, directed by Bill Davis and Bob Boatman, CBS, The Nashville Network, 1969-1997.

Cymbala, Jim, *Fresh Wind, Fresh Fire: What Happens When God's Spirit Invades the Hearts of His People* (Grand Rapids: Zondervan, 1997), 25.

Ibid, 29.

Garrett, Duane A., *The New American Commentary, Volume 14: Proverbs, Ecclesiastes, Song of Songs.* (Broadman Press, Nashville, TN, 1993.), 311.

"Help Babies and Mothers Starting Out." Help Babies and Mothers Survive. Accessed November 7, 2019. https://www.compassion.com/help-mothers-babies-in-poverty.htm.

Lyrics.com, STANDS4 LLC, 2019. "Trust His Heart Lyrics." Accessed November 7, 2019. https://www.lyrics.com/lyric/5061801/Babbie+Mason.

Nixon, Richard M., *RN: The Memoirs of Richard Nixon* (New York: Simon & Schuster, Inc., 1978), 496.

"Our Approach to Prison Ministry." Prison Fellowship. Accessed November 7, 2019. https://www.prisonfellowship.org/about/.

Scriven, Joseph. "What a Friend We have in Jesus." Public domain.

Spurgeon, Charles Haddon. Accessed November 7, 2019. https://www.spurgeon.org/resource-library/sermons/a-happy-christian#flipbook/.

Swindoll, Charles R., *Job: A Man of Heroic Endurance* (Nashville: The W Publishing Group, 2004), 275.

Swindoll, Charles R., *Swindoll's Ultimate Book of Illustrations & Quotes.* (Nashville, TN: Thomas Nelson, 1998), 440-441.

Tolkien, J.R.R., *The Lord of the Rings Trilogy* (London: Allen & Unwin, 1954-1955).